Patchwork Quilting

Nana's Cups & Saucers, page 81

www.companyscoming.com
visit our website

Front Cover: Flower Garden Square, page 96

Patchwork Quilting

Third Printing March 2009

Library and Archives Canada Cataloguing in Publication
Patchwork Quilting.
Includes index.
ISBN 978-1-897069-77-6
1. Quilting. 2. Patchwork quilts.
TT835.P38 2008   746.46   C2007-905522-2

Published by
Company's Coming Publishing Limited
2311-96 Street
Edmonton, Alberta, Canada T6N 1G3
Tel: 780-450-6223 Fax: 780-450-1857
www.companyscoming.com

Printed in Malaysia

THE COMPANY'S COMING STORY

Jean Paré grew up with an understanding that family, friends and home cooking are the key ingredients for a good life. A mother of four, Jean worked as a professional caterer for eighteen years, operating out of her home kitchen. During that time, she came to appreciate quick and easy recipes that call for everyday ingredients. In answer to mounting requests for her recipes, Company's Coming cookbooks were born, and Jean moved on to a new chapter in her career.

Company's Coming founder Jean Paré

In the beginning, Jean worked from a spare bedroom in her home, located in the small prairie town of Vermilion, Alberta, Canada. The first Company's Coming cookbook, 150 Delicious Squares, was an immediate bestseller. Today, with well over 100 titles in print, Company's Coming has earned the distinction of being the publisher of Canada's most popular cookbooks. The company continues to gain new supporters by adhering to Jean's 'Golden Rule of Cooking'—never share a recipe you wouldn't use yourself. It's an approach that works—millions of times over!

Company's Coming cookbooks are distributed throughout Canada, the United States, Australia and other international English-language markets. French and Spanish language editions have also been published. Sales to date have surpassed 25 million copies with no end in sight. Familiar and trusted in home kitchens around the world, Company's Coming cookbooks are highly regarded both as kitchen workbooks and as family heirlooms.

Just as Company's Coming continues to promote the tradition of home cooking, now the same is true with crafting. Like cooking, successful crafts depend upon easy-to-follow instructions, readily available materials and enticing photographs of the finished products. Also like cooking, crafts are meant to be enjoyed in the home or cottage. Company's Coming Crafts, then, seems to be a natural extension from the kitchen into the family room or den.

Because Company's Coming operates a test kitchen and not a craft shop, we've partnered with a major North American craft publisher to assemble a variety of craft compilations exclusively for us. Our editors have been involved every step of the way. You can see the results for yourself in the book you're holding.

Company's Coming Crafts are for everyone—whether you're a beginner or a seasoned pro. What better gift could you offer than something you've made yourself? In these hectic days, people still enjoy crafting parties—whether it be knitting, card making, quilting or any of a wide range of crafts. Crafting brings family and friends together in the same way that a good meal tightens the bond between family and friends. Company's Coming is proud to support crafters with this new craft book series.

We hope you enjoy these easy-to-follow, informative, colourful books and that they will inspire your creativity! So don't delay—get crafty!

TABLE OF CONTENTS

Between the Covers 6 • Foreword 7 • General Instructions 8

Home Quilting

Fill your home with touches of quilting, including tea cozies, coasters and hot pads, just right for tea time or snack time.

Patchwork Table Toppers

Give your tables a new look with quilted table runners and mats; they change easily, so make one for every occasion.

Quilts for Babies to Teens

Quickly quilt a cuddly teddy bear quilt, birthday banner, blue jean quilt and more for your favourite young person.

Denim Table Runner, page 52

Tea for Two, page 18

Sunflower Lane, page 45

New Year's Coaster Set, page 25

Teddy Bear Quilt & Tote, page 56

TABLE OF CONTENTS

Quick Wall Quilts

Create wall quilts that reflect your hobbies, interests and favourite colours; they add warmth and beauty to any room.

Cozy Throws

Lovingly stitch casual and comfy throws to decorate your home; they also make great gifts for friends and family.

Beautiful Bed Quilts

Grace your beds with quilts that reflect your warm, friendly home, quilts you'll love to make and give as gifts.

Prairie Points
Throw, page 122

Secret Garden,
page 92

Tossed Triangles,
page 116

Graceful Baskets,
page 138

Between the Covers

Four Seasons, page 113

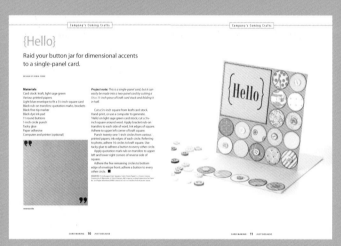

{Hello}, page 10

Counterpane Log Afghan, page 120

Patchwork Quilting

Quilting is a centuries-old tradition that has been resurrected in modern-age popularity. We present you with some of the most colourful and lovely patterns any quilter would be proud to create. There was a great revival of quilting in the 1920s and its popularity continued through the depression. It is again one of the most popular crafts. Patchwork Quilting will help you create a stitch in time!

Card Making
Handmade Greetings for All Occasions

With every card you make, you truly give a bit of yourself in the process. Making your own cards is a fun, creative and less costly way of letting someone know how you really feel. Have you ever looked at a handmade card and thought to yourself, "this is really lovely! I wish I knew how to make my own greeting cards." Well now you can! Making greeting cards is truly fun with Card Making as your guide. Buy it now and we'll show you how!

Knitting
Easy Fun for Everyone

Knitting has enjoyed a surge in popularity over the last few years as more people take up a craft that was once thought of as grandma's hobby. Knitting allows you to make all sorts of useful and beautiful things with a couple needles and some yarn. It's also a great way to occupy your hands while talking, watching a movie or doing almost anything. For beautiful projects, our knitting book is a must have to expand your purls of wisdom!

For more information about Company's Coming craft books, visit our website, www.companyscoming.com

FOREWORD

Take out your box of fabric scraps and plan to spend the weekend quilting. Make a small project that will add a touch of quilting to your family room or dining area. Or make a wall quilt to give as a gift to that special friend.

As you flip through the pages of our book, you'll want to start making blocks for a beautiful bed quilt. Whether you make the quilt for your own home or to give to a loved one, we can guarantee that you'll enjoy each minute as you stitch the quilt. You'll also enjoy the quilt for years to come when you see it is used as a bed cover, adding a warm, loving touch to any bed that it graces.

Creating a cozy throw to wrap around yourself as you watch television or listen to CDs will also bring you hours of stitching pleasure. Everyone in the family will want one to snuggle up in. We don't think you can make too many throws for any family!

For many people, quilts are a work of art. Their favourite place for a quilt is on a wall. A wall quilt can easily become the focal point of any room. Use the quilt design as the starting point, select fabric in the colours you want to use for that room, add or make a few accent pieces in the same colours or fabrics, and your room is finished.

If you don't have much time to quilt, you can still add quilted touches to your home. Table runners and mats can be used in almost any room—as runners on the dining room table or on a coffee table, as a dresser scarf in the bedroom or as a cover for a toy box, piano bench or old-time trunk.

Even quicker projects include tea cozies, coasters and hot pads to use during your afternoon tea or as a housewarming gift for a favourite friend or

relative. They're fun to make and are sure to draw an appreciative comment from everyone who sees them.

So, begin with the most difficult part of all, deciding which project you want to start with. After that, just select your fabric and enjoy your quilting. No matter which project you select, you're sure to enjoy every moment spent quilting. What better time to start than now?

Come Rain or Shine, page 68

GENERAL INSTRUCTIONS

Quilt-Making Basics

Materials & Supplies
Fabrics
One hundred per cent cotton fabrics are recommended for making quilts. Fabrics may be prewashed, depending on your preference. Whether you prewash or not, be sure your fabrics are colourfast and won't run onto each other when washed after use.

Fabrics are woven with threads going in a crosswise and lengthwise direction. The threads cross at right angles—the more threads per inch, the stronger the fabric.

The crosswise threads will stretch a little. The lengthwise threads will not stretch at all. Cutting the fabric at a 45-degree angle to the crosswise and lengthwise threads produces a bias edge which stretches a great deal when pulled (Figure 1).

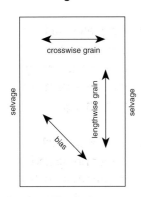 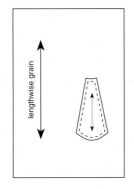

Figure 1   **Figure 2**

If templates are given with patterns in this book, pay careful attention to the grain lines marked with arrows. These arrows indicate that the piece should be placed on the lengthwise grain with the arrow running on one thread (Figure 2).

Thread
For most piecing, good-quality cotton or cotton-covered polyester is the thread of choice. Inexpensive polyester threads are not recommended because they can cut the fibres of cotton fabrics.

Choose a colour thread that will match or blend with the fabrics in your quilt. For projects pieced with dark or light-coloured fabrics choose a neutral thread colour, such as a medium grey, as a compromise between colours. Test by pulling a sample seam.

Batting
Batting is the material used to give a quilt loft or thickness. It also adds warmth.

Some qualities to look for in batting are drapeability, resistance to fibre migration, loft and softness.

Tools & Equipment
There are few truly essential tools and little equipment required for quilt making. Basics include needles (hand-sewing and quilting betweens), pins (long, thin, sharp pins are best), sharp scissors or shears, a thimble, template materials (plastic or cardboard), marking tools (chalk marker, water-erasable pen and a No. 2 pencil are a few) and a quilting frame or hoop. For piecing and/or quilting by machine, add a sewing machine to the list.

Other sewing basics such as a seam ripper, pincushion, measuring tape and an iron are also necessary. For making strip-pieced quilts, a rotary cutter, mat and speciality rulers are often used.

Construction Methods
Traditional Templates. There are two types—templates that include a ¼" seam allowance and those that don't.

Choose the template material and the pattern. Transfer the pattern shapes to the template material with a sharp No. 2 lead pencil. Write the pattern name, piece letter or number, grain line and number to cut for one block or whole quilt on each piece as shown in Figure 3.

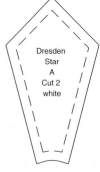

Dresden Star A Cut 2 white

Figure 3

Some patterns require a reversed piece (Figure 4). These patterns are labelled with an R after the piece letter; for example, B and BR. To reverse a template, first cut it with the labelled side up and then with the labelled side down. Or place two layers of fabric with right sides together and cut two pieces at once; one will be reversed.

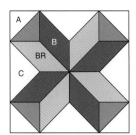

Figure 4

Hand-Piecing Basics. When hand-piecing, it is easier to begin with templates that do not include the ¼" seam allowance. Place the template on the wrong side of the fabric, lining up the marked grain line with lengthwise or crosswise fabric grain. Trace around shape; move, leaving ½" between the shapes, and mark again.

When you have marked the appropriate number of pieces, cut out pieces, leaving ¼" beyond marked line all around each piece.

To join two units, place the patches with right sides together. Stick a pin in at the beginning of the seam through both fabric patches, matching the beginning points (Figure 5); for hand-piecing, the seam begins on the traced line, not at the edge of the fabric (see Figure 6).

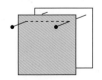

Figure 5   **Figure 6**

Thread a sharp needle; knot one strand of the thread at the end. Remove the pin and insert the needle in the hole; make a short stitch and then

a backstitch right over the first stitch. Continue making short stitches with several stitches on the needle at one time. As you stitch, check the back piece often to assure accurate stitching on the seam line. Take a stitch at the end of the seam; backstitch and knot at the same time as shown in Figure 7. Seams on hand-pieced fabric patches may be finger-pressed toward the darker fabric.

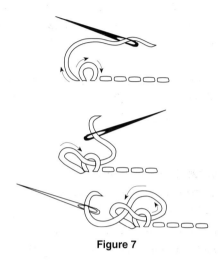

Figure 7

Machine-Piecing. If making templates, include the ¼" seam allowance on the template for machine-piecing. Place template on the wrong side of the fabric as for hand-piecing except butt pieces against one another when tracing.

Set machine on 2.5 or 12–15 stitches per inch. Join pieces as for hand-piecing, beginning and ending sewing at the end of the fabric patch. No backstitching is necessary when machine-stitching.

Quick-Cutting. Templates can be completely eliminated when using a rotary cutter with a plastic ruler and mat to cut fabric strips.

When rotary-cutting strips, straighten raw edges of fabric by folding fabric in fourths across the width as shown in Figure 8. Press down flat; place ruler on fabric square with edge of fabric and make one cut from the folded edge to the outside edge. If strips are not straightened, a wavy strip will result as shown in Figure 9.

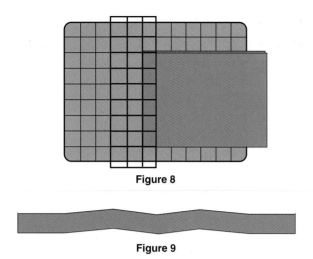

Figure 8

Figure 9

Always cut away from your body, holding the ruler firmly with the non-cutting hand.

Quick-Piecing Method. Lay pieces to be joined under the presser foot of the sewing machine right sides together. Sew an exact ¼" seam allowance to the end of the piece; place another unit right next to the first one and continue sewing, adding a piece after every stitched piece, until all of the pieces are used up (Figure 10).

Figure 10

When sewing is finished, cut the threads that join the pieces apart. Press seam toward the darker fabric.

Appliqué
Making Templates. The appliqué designs given in this book are shown as full-size drawings. The drawings show dotted lines to indicate where one piece overlaps another. Other marks indicate placement of embroidery stitches for decorative purposes such as eyes, lips, flowers, etc.

Before the actual appliqué process begins, cut the background block.

Transfer the design to a large piece of tracing paper. Using a light box, transfer design to fabric background.

If you don't have a light box, tape the pattern on a window; centre the background block on top and tape in place. Trace the design onto the background block with a water-erasable marker, or light lead or chalk pencil. This drawing will mark exactly where the fabric pieces should be placed on the background block.

Hand Appliqué. Traditional hand appliqué uses a template made from the desired finished shape without seam allowance added.

After fabric is prepared, trace the desired shape onto the right side of the fabric with a water-erasable marker, or light lead or chalk pencil. Leave at least ½" between design motifs when tracing to allow for the seam allowance when cutting out the shapes.

When the desired number of shapes needed has been drawn on the fabric pieces, cut out shapes leaving ⅛"–¼" all around drawn line for turning under.

Turn the shape's edges over on the drawn or stitched line. When turning in concave curves, clip to seams and baste the seam allowance over as shown in Figure 11.

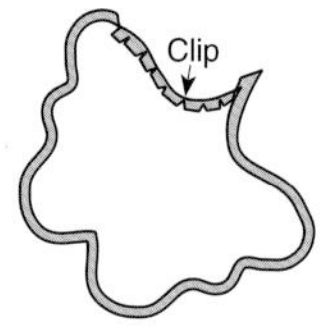

Figure 11

For hand appliqué, position the fabric shapes on the background block and pin or baste them in place. Using a blind stitch or appliqué stitch, sew pieces in place with matching thread and small stitches. Start with background pieces first and work up to foreground pieces.

Machine Appliqué. There are several products available to help make the machine-appliqué process easier and faster.

Fusible transfer web is a commercial product similar to iron-on interfacings except it has two sticky sides. It is used to adhere appliqué shapes to the background with heat. Paper is adhered to one side of the web.

To use, reverse pattern and draw shapes onto the paper side of the web; cut, leaving a margin around each shape. Place on the wrong side of the chosen fabric; fuse in place referring to the manufacturer's instructions. Cut out shapes on the drawn line. Peel off the paper and fuse in place on the background fabric. Transfer any detail lines to the fabric shapes.

Putting It All Together

Finishing the Top
Settings. Most quilts are made by sewing individual blocks together in rows that, when joined, create a design.

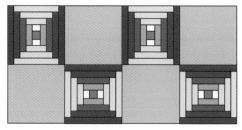

Figure 1

Plain blocks can be alternated with pieced or appliquéd blocks in a straight set. (Figure 1)

Adding Borders. Borders are an integral part of the quilt and should complement the colours and designs used in the quilt centre.

If fabric strips are added for borders, they may be mitred (Figure 2) or butted (Figure 3) at the corners. To determine the size for butted border strips, measure across the centre of the completed quilt top from one side raw edge to the other side raw edge. This measurement will include a ¼" seam allowance.

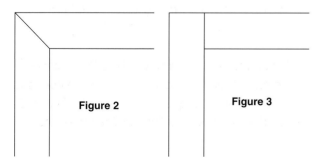

Figure 2   **Figure 3**

Cut two border strips that length by the chosen width of the border. Sew these strips to the top and bottom of the pieced centre referring to Figure 4. Press the seam allowance toward the border strips.

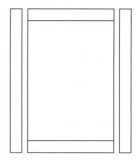

Figure 4

Measure across the completed quilt top at the centre, from top raw edge to bottom raw edge, including the two border strips already added. Cut two border strips that length by the chosen width of the border. Sew a strip to each of the two remaining sides as shown in Figure 4. Press the seams toward the border strips.

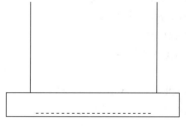

Figure 5

To make mitred corners, measure the quilt as before. Multiply the width of the border by two. Add this amount to the quilt measurement and ½" for seam allowances to determine the length of the strips. Repeat for opposite sides. Sew on each strip, stopping stitching ¼" from corner (Figure 5), leaving the remainder of the strip dangling.

Press corners at a 45-degree angle to form a crease (Figure 6). Stitch from the inside quilt corner to the outside on the creased line. Trim excess away after stitching and press mitred seams open (Figures 7).

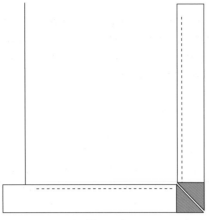

Figure 6

Figure 10

Meander or free-motion quilting by machine fills in open spaces and doesn't require marking. It is fun and easy to stitch as shown in Figure 10.

Press seam open

Figure 7

Marking the Top for Quilting. If you choose a fancy or allover design for quilting, you will need to transfer the design to your quilt top before layering with the backing and batting. You may use a sharp medium-lead or silver pencil on light background fabrics. Test the pencil marks to guarantee that they will wash out of your quilt top when quilting is complete; or be sure your quilting stitches cover the pencil marks. Mechanical pencils with very fine points may be used successfully to mark quilts.

Getting Ready to Quilt

Choosing a Quilting Design. There are several types of quilting designs, some of which may not have to be marked. The easiest of the unmarked designs is in-the-ditch quilting. Here the quilting stitches are placed in the valley created by the seams joining two pieces together or next to the edge of an appliqué design. (Figure 8).

Preparing the Quilt Backing. A backing is generally cut at least 4" larger than the quilt top or 2" larger on all sides. For a 64" x 78" finished quilt, the backing would need to be at least 68" x 82."

To avoid having the seam across the centre of the quilt backing, cut or tear one of the right-length pieces in half and sew half to each side of the second piece as shown in Figure 11.

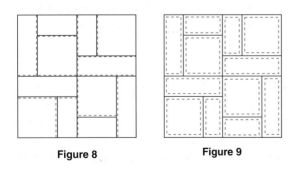

Figure 8   **Figure 9**

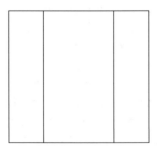

Figure 11

Outline-quilting ¼" or more away from seams or appliqué shapes is another no-mark alternative (Figure 9) that prevents having to sew through the layers made by seams, thus making stitching easier.

Layering the Quilt Sandwich. Open the batting several days before you need it, to help flatten the creases caused from its being folded up in the bag for so long. Iron the backing piece.

To hold the quilt layers together for quilting, baste by hand or use safety pins. If basting by hand, thread a long thin needle with a long piece of unknotted white or off-white thread. Starting in the centre and leaving a long tail, make 4"–6" stitches toward the outside edge of the quilt top, smoothing as you baste. Start at the centre again and work toward the outside as shown in Figure 12.

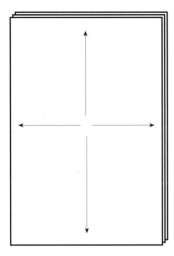

Figure 12

If quilting by machine, you may prefer to use safety pins for holding your fabric sandwich together. Start in the centre of the quilt and pin to the outside, leaving pins open until all are placed. When you are satisfied that all layers are smooth, close the pins.

Quilting

Hand Quilting. To begin, thread a sharp between needle with an 18" piece of quilting thread. Tie a small knot in the end of the thread. Position the needle about ½" to 1" away from the starting point on quilt top. Sink the needle through the top into the batting layer but not through the backing. Pull the needle up at the starting point of the quilting design. Pull the needle and thread until the knot sinks through the top into the batting (Figure 13).

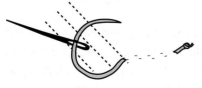

Figure 13

Take small, even running stitches along the marked quilting line. Keep one hand positioned underneath to feel the needle go all the way through to the backing.

When you have nearly run out of thread, wind the thread around the needle several times to make a small knot and pull it close to the fabric. Insert the needle into the fabric on the quilting line and come out with the needle ½" to 1" away, pulling the knot into the fabric layers the same as when you started. Pull and cut thread close to fabric. The end should disappear inside after cutting. Some quilters prefer to take a backstitch with a loop through it for a knot to end.

Machine Quilting. Successful machine quilting requires practice and a good relationship with your sewing machine.

Prepare the quilt for machine quilting in the same way as for hand quilting. Use safety pins to hold the layers together.

Set the machine on a longer stitch length (3.0 or 8–10 stitches to the inch). An even-feed or walking foot helps to eliminate tucks and puckering by feeding the upper and lower layers through the machine evenly. Before you begin, loosen the amount of pressure on the presser foot.

Special machine-quilting needles work best to penetrate the three layers in your quilt.

Finishing the Edges

Binding. To prepare the quilt for the addition of the binding, trim the batting and backing layers flush with the top of the quilt. Using a walking-foot attachment (sometimes called an even-feed foot attachment), machine-baste the three layers together all around approximately ⅛" from the cut edge.

The materials listed for each quilt often includes a number of yards of self-made or purchased binding. The advantage to self-made binding is that you can use fabrics from your quilt to co-ordinate colours.

Double-fold, straight-grain binding is used on projects with right-angle corners. To make this binding, cut 2¼"-wide strips of fabric across the width or down the length of the fabric totalling the perimeter of the quilt plus 10." The strips are joined as shown in Figure 14 and pressed in half wrong sides together along the length using an iron on a cotton setting with no steam.

Figure 14

Lining up the raw edges, place the binding on the top of the quilt and begin sewing (again using the walking foot) approximately 6" from the beginning of the binding strip. Stop sewing ¼" from the first corner, leave the needle in the quilt, turn and sew diagonally to the corner as shown in Figure 15.

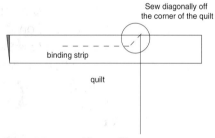

Sew diagonally off the corner of the quilt

binding strip

quilt

Figure 15

Fold the binding at a 45-degree angle up and away from the quilt as shown in Figure 16 and back down flush with the raw edges. Starting at the top raw edge of the quilt, begin sewing the next side as shown in Figure 17. Repeat at the next three corners.

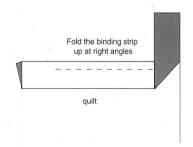

Fold the binding strip up at right angles

quilt

Figure 16

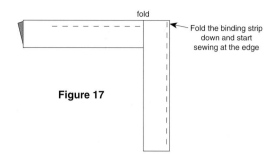

fold

Fold the binding strip down and start sewing at the edge

Figure 17

As you approach the beginning of the binding strip, stop stitching and overlap the binding ½" from the edge; trim. Join the two ends with a ¼" seam allowance and press the seam open. Reposition the joined binding along the edge of the quilt and resume stitching to the beginning.

To finish, bring the folded edge of the binding over the raw edges and blind-stitch the binding in place over the machine-stitching line on the back side. Hand-mitre the corners on the back as shown in Figure 18.

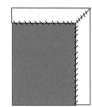

Figure 18

Adding a Sleeve

To make a sleeve, measure across the top of the finished quilt. Cut an 8"-wide piece of muslin equal to that length.

Fold in ¼" on each end of the muslin strip and press. Fold again and stitch to hold. Fold the muslin strip lengthwise with right sides together. Sew along the long side to make a tube. Turn the tube right side out; press with seam at bottom or centred on the back.

Hand-stitch the tube along the top of the quilt and the bottom of the tube to the quilt back. Stitches should not go through to the front of the quilt.

Slip a wooden dowel or long curtain rod through the sleeve to hang.

When the quilt is finally complete, it should be signed and dated. Use a permanent pen on the back of the quilt.

Tea Cozy & Coaster Set

Sew these pretty co-ordinates to make tea time a special event.

BY MARIAN SHENK

Project Specifications
Skill Level: Beginner
Tea Cozy Size: Approximately 4" x 14" x 4"
   (adjustable to fit most teapots)
Coaster Size: 4" diameter (includes binding)

Materials
- ¼ yard each of four co-ordinating prints
- ⅓ yard contrasting print for lining and drawstring
- ⅓ yard thin batting
- All-purpose thread to blend with fabrics
- Rotary-cutting tools

Instructions

Tea Cozy
Step 1. Cut 20 assorted strips 1½" x 12" from four co-ordinating fabrics and contrasting print. Piece together on long edges to make two rectangles 10½" x 12." Press all seam allowances in one direction.

Step 2. From batting and contrasting print cut two rectangles each 10½" x 12." Place one contrasting print lining and one pieced rectangle right sides together with one batting piece on top. Sew both long edges for front of tea cozy. Turn right side out. Repeat for back of tea cozy. Machine-quilt in the ditch of seams on each piece.

Step 3. Cut six assorted strips 1¼" x 21" from four co-ordinating fabrics and contrasting print. Piece together on long edges to make a rectangle 5" x 21." Press all seam allowances in one direction.

Step 4. Cut a 4½" circle from pieced rectangle, batting and lining fabric. Layer and quilt in the ditch of seams.

Step 5. Right sides of tea cozy facing, sew front to back 3" up from the bottom on each side. Sew 1½" down from the top on one side only. The opening between will be for insertion of teapot spout.

Step 6. Gather bottom edges of tea cozy to fit the 4½" quilted circle and sew. Turn tea cozy right side out.

Step 7. From contrasting print cut two strips 9¾" x 1¾." Turn under ¼" on short ends and one long side of each piece. With wrong side of one strip facing right side of front lining, align raw edge of strip with top edge of tea cozy front. Pin in place. Topstitch through all layers close to folded long edge. Repeat on tea cozy back.

Step 8. From contrasting print, cut two strips 5" x 10½." Fold in half lengthwise, right sides together, and sew short ends. Turn right side out and sew strips to top of front and back of tea cozy, enclosing raw edge of strip added in Step 7. This will create a casing.

Step 9. From contrasting print cut a strip 1½" x 32." Fold in half lengthwise, right sides facing, and sew long edge. Turn right side out and press with seam centred on back of strip. Thread through casing and tie a knot in each end.

Coasters
Step 1. From rectangle sewn in Tea Cozy, Step 3, cut four 4" circles. From contrasting print and batting cut four 4" circles each. Layer for each

coaster and machine-quilt in the ditch of each piece and perpendicular to seams in a ¾" grid.

Step 2. From contrasting print make 2 yards of 2¼"-wide bias binding, referring to General Instructions. Bind each coaster to finish. ◆

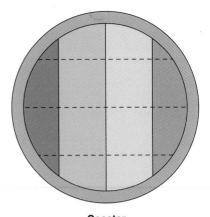

Coaster
Placement Diagram
4" Diameter (includes binding)

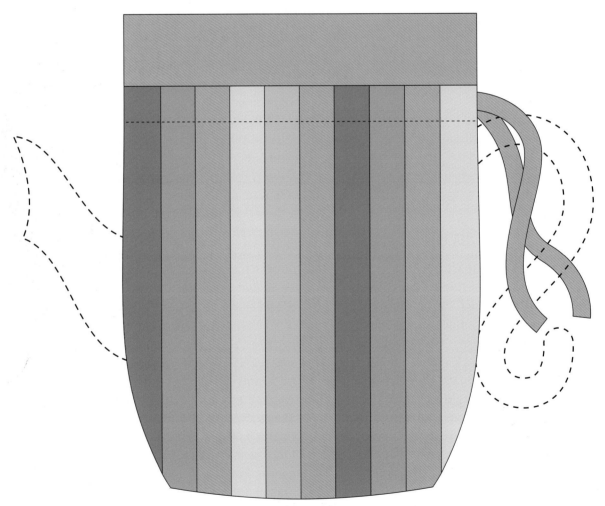

Tea Cozy
Placement Diagram
Approximately 4" x 14" x 4"

Tea for Two

When the temperature plummets we want tea hot and bracing. This warm little cover will ensure a hot beverage.

BY BETTY ALDERMAN

Project Specifications
Skill Level: Beginner
Tea Cozy Size: 9" x 12"

Materials
- Scraps for teapot appliqué
- ¼ yard contrasting fabric for trim, binding and loop
- ½ yard background fabric
- ½ yard lining
- Batting 18" x 40"
- Machine embroidery thread to match or contrast with appliqué
- 1 spool quilting thread to blend with background fabric
- 1 yard purchased piping to match trim and binding
- ¼ yard fusible transfer web

Instructions
Step 1. Cut tea cozy pieces from fabric as directed on pattern.
Step 2. Trace appliqué shapes onto paper side of fusible transfer web; cut out, leaving ½" margin around shapes.
Step 3. Fuse to wrong side of selected fabrics and cut out on tracing line.
Step 4. Position teapot pieces on right side of one of the background pieces, referring to Placement Diagram, and fuse in place according to manufacturer's directions. Machine appliqué, referring to General Instructions.

Step 5. Layer one each, tea cozy background, batting and lining, and quilt by hand or machine; repeat.
Step 6. Trace the tea cozy pattern onto lining side of appliquéd piece as shown in Figure 1. Place the two quilted pieces right sides together and cut out on traced line through all layers as shown in Figure 2.

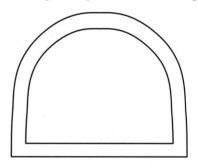

Figure 1

Figure 2

Step 7. Following appliqué directions in Steps 2–4, add sawtooth border to bottom edges of both quilted pieces.
Step 8. Cut a strip of contrasting fabric 1" x 3." Fold long edges to centre and fold again as shown in

Figure 3. Edge-stitch along long edge. Fold in half to form loop and place loop on right side at centre top of tea cozy front.

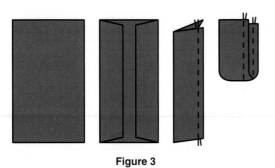

Figure 3

Step 9. Baste purchased piping to front of tea cozy along curved edge, matching raw edges. Extend piping ½" beyond lower edges.

Step 10. Place front and back of tea cozy right

sides together. Using zipper foot, stitch around curved edge of cozy close to piping. Clip curve, turn right side out and trim piping even with bottom edge as shown in Figure 4.

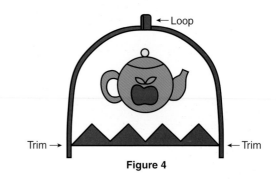

Figure 4

Step 11. Make bias binding 1¼" x 30" from contrasting fabric and apply to bottom edge, referring to General Instructions. ◆

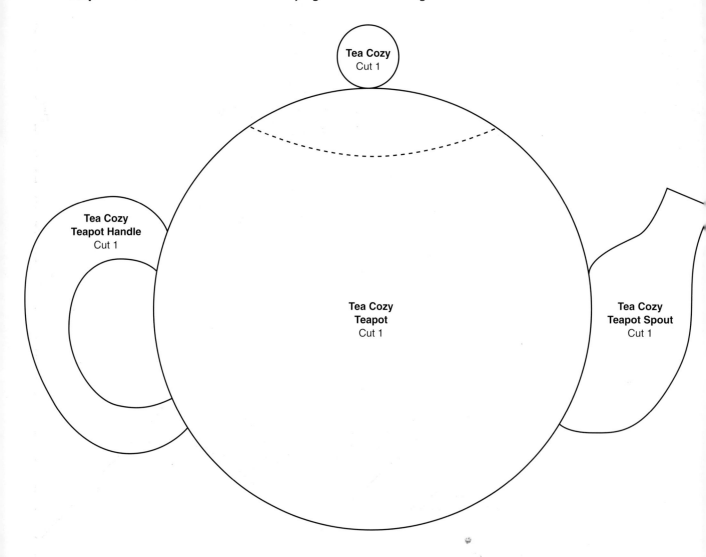

Tea Cozy
Cut 1

Tea Cozy
Teapot Handle
Cut 1

Tea Cozy
Teapot
Cut 1

Tea Cozy
Teapot Spout
Cut 1

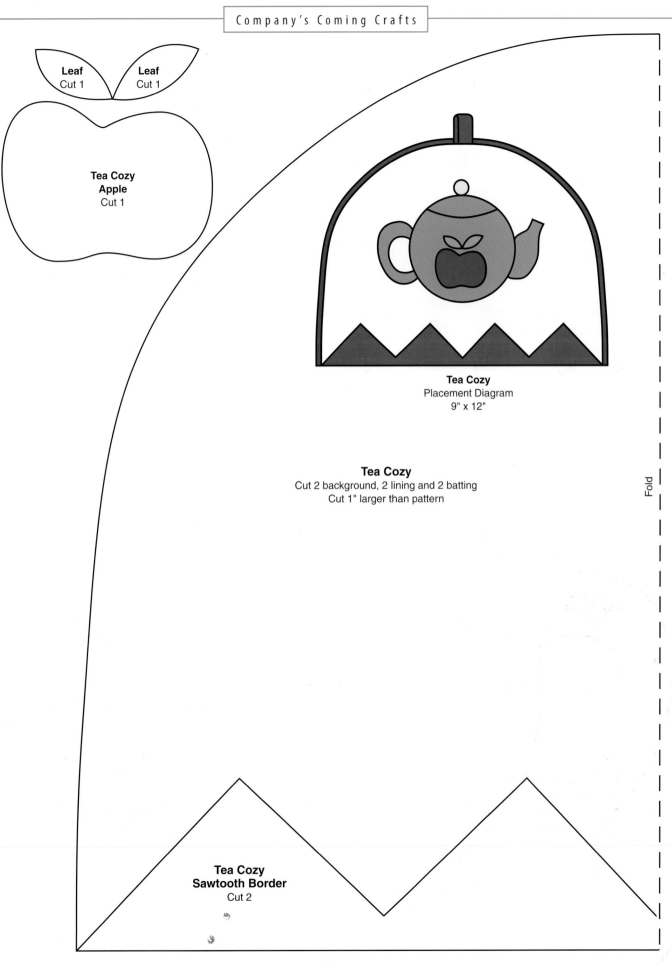

Leaf
Cut 1

Leaf
Cut 1

**Tea Cozy
Apple**
Cut 1

Tea Cozy
Placement Diagram
9" x 12"

Tea Cozy
Cut 2 background, 2 lining and 2 batting
Cut 1" larger than pattern

Fold

**Tea Cozy
Sawtooth Border**
Cut 2

Log Cabin Coaster Set

Log placement makes this quartet matching but different.

BY RUTH SWASEY

Project Specifications

Skill Level: Beginner
Coaster Size: 4¾" x 4¾"

Materials

- Scraps of yellow and blue prints
- ⅓ yard multicoloured print for centre, backing and binding
- 4 pieces thin cotton batting 5¼" x 5¼"
- All-purpose thread to blend with fabrics
- 1 spool yellow quilting thread
- Rotary-cutting tools

Instructions

Hour Glass

Step 1. From blue and yellow prints cut two strips each 1" x 16." Sew alternate strips together and cut into triangles as shown in Figure 1.

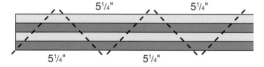

Figure 1

Step 2. Cut one square of multicoloured print 1¼" x 1¼." Sew one triangle to each side of centre square as shown in Figure 2.

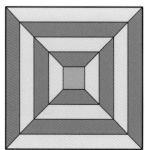

Figure 2

Sunshine & Shadow

Step 1. Cut blue and yellow prints into 1" strips. Cut one square of multicoloured print 1¼" x 1¼."

Step 2. Sew a yellow strip to centre square and trim. Sew another yellow strip and trim. Repeat with two blue strips and continue as numbered in Figure 3.

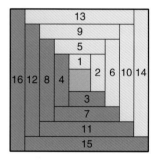

Figure 3

Square Upon Square

Step 1. Cut blue and yellow prints into 1" strips. From multicoloured print cut one square 1¼" x 1¼."

Step 2. Sew yellow strips to each side of centre square. Repeat with blue. Continue as numbered in Figure 4.

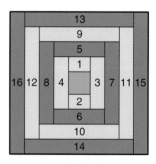

Figure 4

Paper Lantern

Step 1. This block is the same as Square Upon Square, but with different colour placement. Follow placement order as numbered in Figure 5.

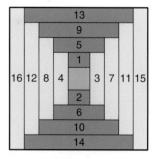

Figure 5

Finishing

Step 1. Press completed blocks. Referring to General Instructions, prepare blocks for quilting. Quilt as desired.

Step 2. For each coaster make a 2¼" x 24" binding strip. Bind to finish, referring to General Instructions. ◆

Hour Glass

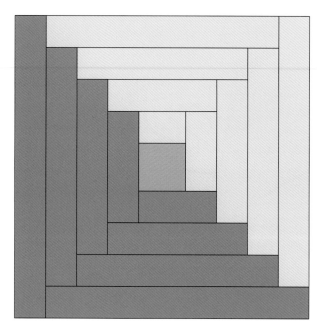

Sunshine & Shadow

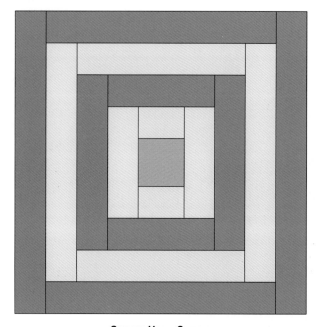

Square Upon Square

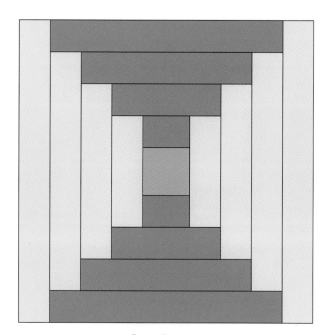

Paper Lantern

Log Cabin Coaster Set
Placement Diagram
Each 4³/₄" x 4³/₄"

New Year's Coaster Set

Colourful coasters are fast and fun to make, adding sparkle to holiday festivities.

BY KATE LAUCOMER

Project Specifications
Skill Level: Beginner
Coaster Size: 4½" x 4½"

Materials
For each coaster
- Variety of scraps
- Backing 4½" x 4½"
- Batting 4½" x 4½"
- 20" piece self-made or purchased binding
- All-purpose thread to blend with patchwork fabrics
- Black, contrasting or variegated embroidery floss
- Gold metallic quilting thread
- Fusible web

Instructions
Step 1. For single-colour backgrounds, cut a 4½" square.

Step 2. For half-square triangle backgrounds, cut 4⅞" squares from each of two fabrics. Draw a diagonal line on the wrong side of one square. Put right sides of two squares together and stitch ¼" on both sides of the diagonal line as shown in Figure 1. Cut on diagonal line and press seams toward darker fabric. Trim resulting squares to 4½" x 4½," if necessary.

Figure 1

Step 3. For four-triangle backgrounds, cut 6¼" squares from two fabrics. Follow directions for half-square triangle, but do not trim. On the back of one half-square block, mark a diagonal line. Put right sides of two blocks together, opposite colours facing each other. Stitch ¼" on both sides of diagonal line. Cut on diagonal line as shown in Figure 2; press seam open. Trim block to 4½," if necessary.

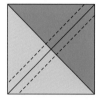

Figure 2

Step 4. See Figures 3–6 for template placement. Trace templates for star of choice on paper side of fusible web. Iron fusible web to back of selected fabric. Cut out each piece exactly on traced lines. Position on background of choice, leaving at least ⅜" between star points and edges of background block. Fuse in place according to manufacturer's directions.

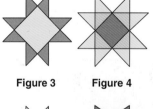

Figure 3   **Figure 4**

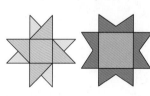

Figure 5   **Figure 6**

Step 5. Buttonhole-stitch around each appliqué piece (and dotted line of template F) with 2 strands of embroidery floss.

Step 6. Layer backing, batting and appliquéd layers. Pin, baste and bind, referring to General Instructions.

Step 7. Hand- or machine-quilt with gold metallic thread. ◆

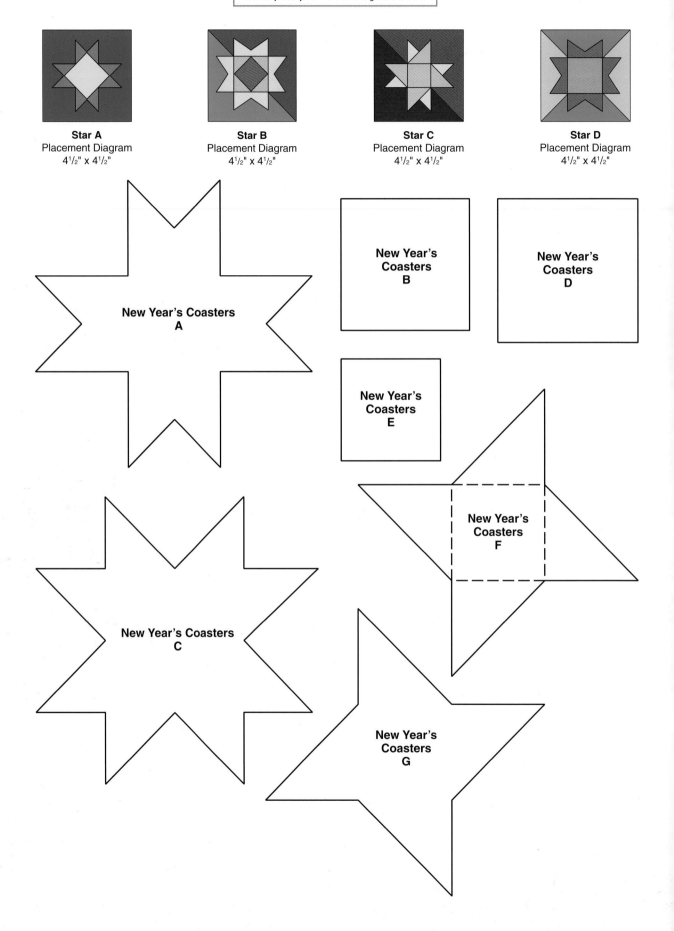

Star A
Placement Diagram
$4^1/_2$" x $4^1/_2$"

Star B
Placement Diagram
$4^1/_2$" x $4^1/_2$"

Star C
Placement Diagram
$4^1/_2$" x $4^1/_2$"

Star D
Placement Diagram
$4^1/_2$" x $4^1/_2$"

New Year's Coasters
A

New Year's
Coasters
B

New Year's
Coasters
D

New Year's
Coasters
E

New Year's
Coasters
F

New Year's Coasters
C

New Year's
Coasters
G

Apples & Cherries

Apples and cherries bring cheer to your kitchen.

BY BARBARA CLAYTON

Project Specifications
Skill Level: Beginner
Block Size: 8" x 8"

Materials
- ⅓ yard white solid
- ⅜ yard blue-and-white print
- ¾ yard blue dot
- Scraps red dot, red solid, green solid and green print
- 2 squares batting 8½" x 8½"
- 6" x 6" square fabric stabilizer
- 8" x 8" square medium-weight fusible interfacing
- 1 spool each brown and green rayon thread

Instructions
Step 1. Cut two squares white solid 4½" x 4½."
Step 2. Prepare appliqué pieces for one each cherry and apple motif with leaves referring to patterns.
Step 3. Centre a cherry motif on one 4½" x 4½" white square and an apple motif on the other. Appliqué in place. Referring to the Placement Diagram, draw cherry stems and apple stems on background with a water-soluble pen. Machine-zigzag apple stem with brown rayon thread and cherry stems with green rayon thread.
Step 4. Cut one strip each blue dot and white solid 1½" by fabric width on a cutting mat using a rotary cutter and ruler.
Step 5. Sew strips together along length; press seam toward blue dot.

1½"

Figure 1

Step 6. Cut stitched strip into 1½" segments as shown in Figure 1; repeat across strip.
Step 7. Construct two checkerboard strips using four segments in each strip as shown in Figure 2; repeat for eight checkerboard strips (four for each pot holder).

Figure 2

Step 8. Cut eight squares blue-and-white print 2½" x 2½." Sew a checkerboard strip between two squares as shown in Figure 3; repeat for four units.

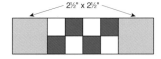

2½" x 2½"

Figure 3

Step 9. Sew a checkerboard strip to opposite sides of each appliquéd square as shown in Figure 4.

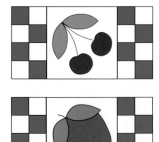

Figure 4

Step 10. Join the pieced sections as shown in Figure 5 to complete pot holder tops.

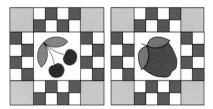

Figure 5

Step 11. Round three corners on each pot holder using pattern provided.

Step 12. Prepare for quilting and quilt as desired.

Step 13. Bind edges and make hanging loop. ✦

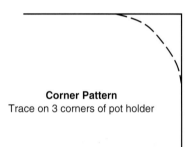

Corner Pattern
Trace on 3 corners of pot holder

Apple
Placement Diagram 8" x 8"

Cherries
Placement Diagram 8" x 8"

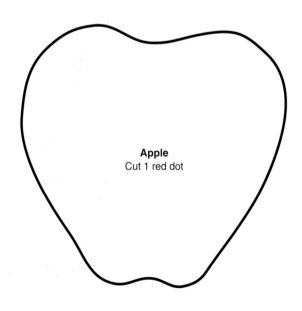

Apple
Cut 1 red dot

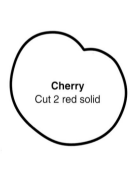

Cherry
Cut 2 red solid

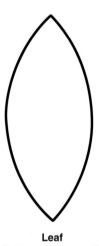

Leaf
Cut 2 each green solid
& green print

Dresden Place Mats & Pot Holders

Fan
8" x 8" x 11¼" Block

Use two Fan blocks to make these simple place mats and pot holders for the kitchen.

BY MARIAN SHENK

Place Mats

Project Specifications
Skill Level: Beginner
Place Mat Size: 13" x 20"
Block Size: 8" x 8" x 11¼" Block
Number of Blocks: 4

Materials
- Fat eighth each 1 green, 2 purple and 3 blue prints
- ¾ yard blue solid
- ⅝ yard cream-on-cream print
- 25" x 34" rectangle batting
- Neutral colour all-purpose thread
- Cream quilting thread
- 1 package blue bias tape

Instructions
Step 1. Prepare template for B using pattern piece given; cut as directed for one Fan block; repeat for four Fan blocks. Prepare template for K using pattern piece given; cut as directed for one Fan block. Repeat for four Fan blocks.
Step 2. Join six K pieces (one of each fat-eighth print fabric) to make a fan shape as shown in Figure 1; press seams in one direction.

Figure 1

Step 3. Centre and set in B as shown in Figure 2 to complete one Fan block; repeat for four blocks.

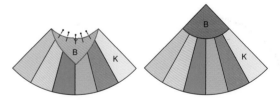

Figure 2

Step 4. Prepare template for H using pattern piece given; cut as directed on piece.
Step 5. Sew a Fan block to the right slanting side of each H piece as shown in Figure 3; press seams toward blocks.

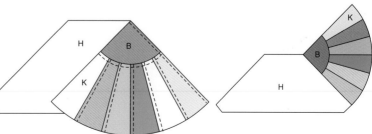

Figure 3

Step 6. Join two pieced units to complete one place mat top as shown in Figure 4; press. Repeat for two place mat tops.

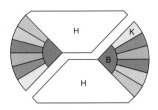

Figure 4

Step 7. Mark completed tops referring to lines on H for quilting.

Step 8. Cut two pieces each batting and blue solid 16" x 23." Sandwich one batting piece between one place-mat top and blue solid backing piece; repeat for two layered sections.

Step 9. Hand-quilt in the ditch of seams of each Fan block and on marked lines using cream quilting thread.

Step 10. Bind edges with blue bias tape; fold over seam and hand-stitch in place on back side to finish.

Dresden Place Mat
Placement Diagram
13" x 20"

Pot Holders

Project Notes

Be sure to use several layers of cotton batting if you want to actually use your pot holders on hot items. Polyester batting will burn easily.

Project Specifications

Skill Level: Beginner
Pot Holder Size: 8" x 8" x 11¼"
Block Size: 8" x 8" x 11¼"
Number of Blocks: 2

Materials

- Fat eighth each 1 green, 2 purple and 3 blue prints
- ⅓ yard blue solid
- 20" x 20" square cotton batting
- Neutral colour all-purpose thread
- Cream quilting thread
- 1 package blue bias tape
- 2 (1") white bone rings

Instructions

Step 1. Prepare template for B using pattern piece given. Cut as directed for one Fan block. Prepare template for K using pattern piece given. Cut as directed for one Fan block.

Step 2. Join six K pieces (one of each fabric) to make a fan shape as shown in Figure 1; press seams in one direction.

Figure 1

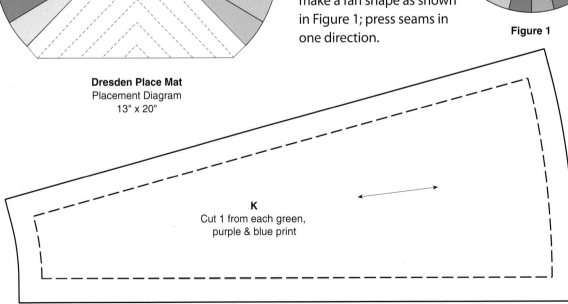

K
Cut 1 from each green,
purple & blue print

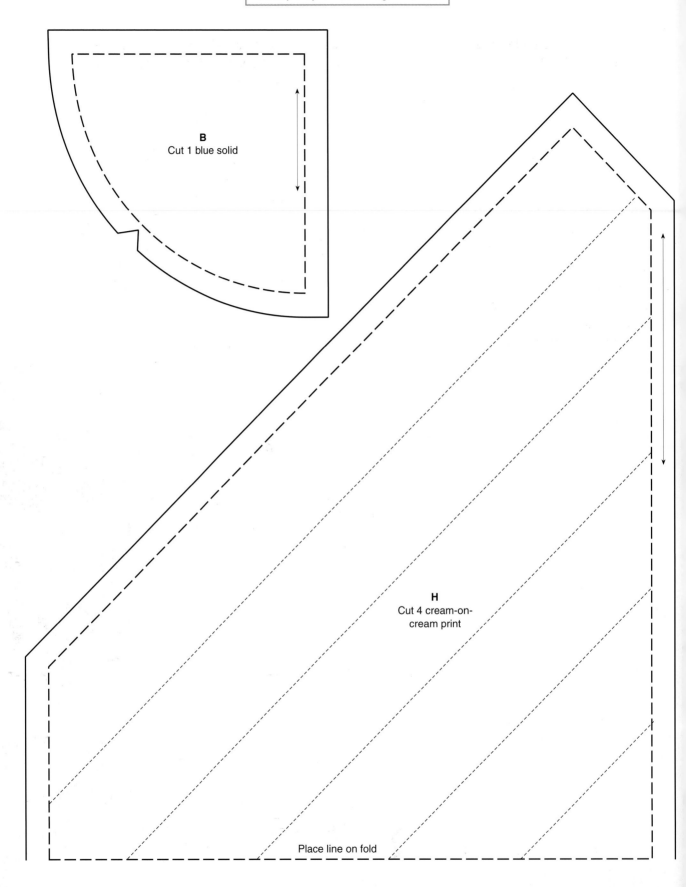

B
Cut 1 blue solid

H
Cut 4 cream-on-
cream print

Place line on fold

Step 3. Centre and set in B as shown in Figure 2 to complete one Fan block.

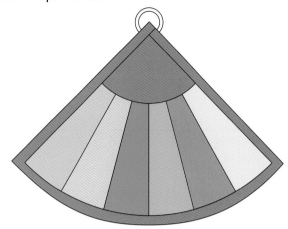

Figure 2

Step 4. Using one pieced block as a pattern, cut two batting and one blue solid lining pieces.

Step 5. Sandwich two batting pieces between one Fan block and one blue solid lining piece.

Step 6. Hand-quilt in the ditch of seams of the Fan block and as desired using cream quilting thread.

Step 7. Bind edges with blue bias tape; fold over seam and hand-stitch in place to enclose seam.

Step 8. Hand-stitch a bone ring to the wrong side at the B-piece end to finish. Repeat to complete a second pot holder. ◆

Dresden Pot Holder
Placement Diagram 8" x 8" x 11¼"

Watermelon Set

A bright watermelon print is the perfect fabric for a summer table set.

BY LUCY A. FAZELY

Project Specifications
Skill Level: Beginner
Runner Size: 50½" x 19½"
Place Mat Size: 19½" x 11¾"
Napkin Size: 19" x 19"

Materials
- ¼ yard pink seed print
- ½ yard green stripe
- ⅝ yard black leaf print
- ⅝ yard black/white stripe
- ⅔ yard cream leaf print
- ⅔ yard red/white check
- Runner backing 56" x 25"
- 2 place mat backings 25" x 18"
- Runner batting 56" x 25"
- 2 place mat battings 25" x 18"
- All-purpose thread to match fabrics
- Clear nylon monofilament

Instructions
Cutting
Step 1. Cut one 7½" by fabric width strip pink seed print; subcut strip into four 7½" A squares. Cut each A square in half on one diagonal to make eight A triangles.

Step 2. Cut one 13" by fabric width strip green stripe; subcut strip into (16) 2½" B strips.

Step 3. Cut two 10" by fabric width strips cream leaf print; subcut strips into eight 10" C squares. Cut each square in half on one diagonal to make 16 C triangles.

Step 4. Cut seven 2½" by fabric width strips black leaf print; set aside three strips for G borders. Subcut remaining strips into two 16" D pieces, four 8¼" E pieces and four 20" F pieces.

Step 5. Cut one 20" by fabric width strip red/white check; subcut into two 20" squares for napkins.

Step 6. Cut eight 2¼" by fabric width strips black/white stripe for binding.

Completing the Runner
Step 1. Separate the B strips into sets of two, matching the stripe colour in each set as much as possible. Sew the lightest side of one B strip to one

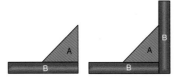
short side of A as shown in Figure 1; press seams toward B. Stitch a second B strip to the adjacent short side of the A-B

Figure 1

unit, again referring to Figure 1; press seam toward B.

Step 2. Trim excess B strips even with A as shown in Figure 2; repeat for eight A-B units.

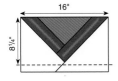

Figure 2

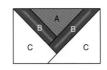

Figure 3

Step 3. Sew a C triangle to each B side of each A-B unit, extending C beyond the point of A-B as shown in Figure 3; press seams toward C.

Step 4. Trim each A-B-C unit to 16" x 8¼" as shown in Figure 4. Set aside two units for place mats.

Figure 4

Figure 5

Step 5. Join three A-B-C units as shown in Figure 5; press seams toward C edges; repeat for two pieced sections.

Step 6. Join the two pieced sections to complete the pieced centre referring to the Placement Diagram for positioning; press seam open.

Step 7. Sew a D strip to opposite ends of the pieced centre; press seams toward D.

Step 8. Join the three G strips on short ends to make one long strip; subcut into two 51" G strips.

Step 9. Sew G to opposite long sides of the pieced centre to complete the runner top; press seams toward G.

Step 10. Sandwich the runner batting between the completed top and prepared runner backing; pin or baste layers together to hold.

Step 11. Machine-quilt as desired using clear nylon monofilament. When quilting is complete, trim batting and backing even with top; remove pins or basting.

Step 12. Join binding strips on short ends to make one long strip. Fold the strip in half along length with wrong sides together; press.

Step 13. Sew binding to runner edges, mitring corners and overlapping ends. Fold binding to the back side and stitch in place to finish. Set aside excess binding for place mats.

Completing Place Mats

Step 1. Sew an E strip to opposite short sides of each remaining A-B-C unit; press seams toward E.

Step 2. Sew an F strip to opposite long sides of the each pieced centre to complete the place mat tops; press seams toward F.

Step 3. Complete place mats as for runner.

Napkins

Step 1. Turn under the edges of each 20" napkin square ¼;" press. Turn under ¼" again; press and stitch to complete napkins. ◆

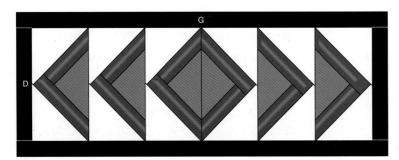

Watermelon Runner
Placement Diagram 50½" x 19½"

Watermelon Place Mat
Placement Diagram 19½" x 11¾"

Sunflower Centrepiece

Make this bright centrepiece using four yellow prints in a Dresden-Plate design to resemble a sunflower.

BY MARIAN SHENK

Quilting Design for B

Project Specifications
Skill Level: Beginner
Project Size: 24" x 24"

Materials
- ¼ yard each 3 yellow prints
- 1 square light yellow print 10" x 10"
- Backing 29" x 29"
- Batting 29" x 29"
- All-purpose thread to match fabrics
- Yellow quilting thread
- ¾ yard 1"-wide white lace
- ¾ yard ½"-wide gold braid

Instructions
Step 1. Prepare templates using pattern pieces given; cut as directed on each piece.

Step 2. Join three different yellow print A pieces as shown in Figure 1; repeat with fabrics in the same order for four A sections.

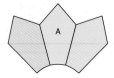

Figure 1

Step 3. Join the pieced A sections to complete a circle; press seams in one direction.

Step 4. Lay pieced section on a flat surface. Centre the B circle piece on top to cover centre hole; hand-baste in place to hold.

Step 5. Pin 1"-wide white lace around edges of circle, overlapping ends slightly; stitch in place.

Step 6. Cover stitching line with the gold braid, butting ends of braid; stitch through the centre of the braid to attach.

Place line on fold

Place line on fold

B
Cut 1 light yellow print

A
Cut 4 each from 3 yellow prints

Step 7. Lay batting on flat surface; lay the backing piece with wrong side on top of batting. Lay the pieced top right sides together with backing.

Step 8. Stitch all around pieced shape using a ¼" seam allowance and leaving a 3" opening on one point; trim batting and backing even with pieced shape, clipping corners and points.

Step 9. Turn right side out through opening; hand-stitch opening closed.

Step 10. Mark quilting lines on A and B pieces referring to pattern and Placement Diagram for positioning. Hand-quilt on marked lines using yellow quilting thread to finish. ✦

Sunflower Centrepiece
Placement Diagram
24" x 24"

Circle of Leaves

The leaf-shaped pieces in this table mat are machine-appliquéd to avoid the challenge of curved piecing.

BY CARLA SCHWAB

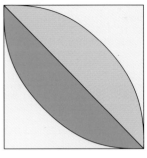

Yellow Leaf
4½" x 4½" Block
Make 32

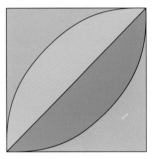

Coral Leaf
4½" x 4½" Block
Make 32

Project Specifications
Skill Level: Intermediate
Project Size: 36" x 36"
Block Size: 4½" x 4½"
Number of Blocks: 64

Materials
- ¾ yard dark green mottled
- ¾ yard each yellow and coral prints
- 1 yard total of a variety of light green prints
- Backing 40" x 40"
- Batting 40" x 40"
- Neutral colour all-purpose thread
- Green variegated rayon thread
- Green quilting thread

Instructions
Step 1. Cut 32 squares each yellow and coral prints 5" x 5."
Step 2. Prepare template for piece A using pattern given. Cut 64 A pieces from the various light green prints.
Step 3. Cut 11 strips dark green mottled 2" by fabric width.
Step 4. Sew the various light green print pieces to the dark green mottled strips, placing right sides together and sewing along the straight edge using a ¼" seam allowance as shown in Figure 1.

Figure 1

Step 5. Using the light green print half as the template, trim away the outside edge of dark green print as shown in Figure 2; press open to make a leaf shape as shown in Figure 3.

Trim

Figure 2

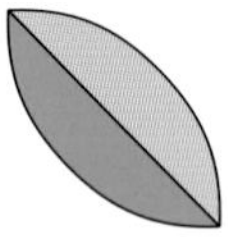

Figure 3

Step 6. Place a leaf shape on each yellow and coral print square as shown in Figure 4; pin in place.

Figure 4

Step 7. Using green variegated rayon thread, machine satin-stitch each leaf shape in place to complete blocks.
Step 8. Join four yellow and four coral blocks to make a row referring to Figure 5; repeat for four rows. Press seams in one direction.

Figure 5

Step 9. Join four coral and four yellow blocks to make a row referring to Figure 6; repeat for four rows. Press seams in one direction.

Figure 6

Step 10. Join the rows referring to the Placement Diagram to complete pieced top; press seams in one direction.

Step 11. Lay quilt top right side up on a flat surface; place prepared backing fabric right sides together with pieced top. Place batting piece on top of backing; pin layers together firmly to hold flat.

Step 12. Stitch around outside edges of quilt, ¼" away from edge of pieced top, leaving a 6" opening right after the corner on one side. Trim excess batting and backing even with pieced top edge.

Step 13. Stitch close to the leaf edge on the centre four-leaf sections of one side as shown in Figure 7; repeat on all four sides. Trim away excess beyond seam as shown in Figure 8.

Figure 7   Figure 8

Step 14. Turn right side out through opening; hand-stitch opening closed.

Step 15. Hand- or machine-quilt close to the edges of each leaf section using green quilting thread to finish. ✦

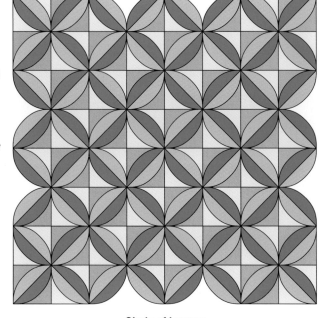

Circle of Leaves
Placement Diagram 36" x 36"

A
Cut 64 from various green prints

Sunflower Lane

The gold colour stands out against the dark triangle units in this simple autumn topper.

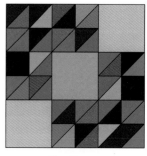

Sunflower
12" x 12" Block

BY NANNETTE BERKLEY

Project Specifications
Skill Level: Beginner
Quilt Size: 34" x 34"
Block Size: 12" x 12"
Number of Blocks: 4

Materials
- Assortment of dark print scraps
- ¼ yard gold tonal
- ⅓ yard navy tonal
- 1 yard green sunflower print

- Backing 40" x 40"
- Batting 40" x 40"
- All-purpose thread to match fabrics
- Quilting thread

Instructions
Cutting
Step 1. Cut (96) 2⅞" x 2⅞" A squares assorted dark prints; mark a diagonal line from corner to corner on the wrong side of 48 of the squares.

Step 2. Cut one 4½" by fabric width strip gold tonal; subcut strip into eight 4½" B squares.

Step 3. Cut four 4½" x 4½" C squares green sunflower print.

Step 4. Cut two 2" x 24½" D strips and two 2" x 27½" E strips navy tonal.

Step 5. Cut two 4" x 27½" F strips and two 4" x 34½" G strips green sunflower print.

Step 6. Cut four 2¼" by fabric width strips green sunflower print for binding.

Piecing the Blocks
Step 1. Place a marked A square right sides together with an unmarked A square. Referring to Figure 1, stitch ¼" on each side of the marked line.

Figure 1

Step 2. Cut the stitched A squares apart on the marked line to make two A units, again referring to

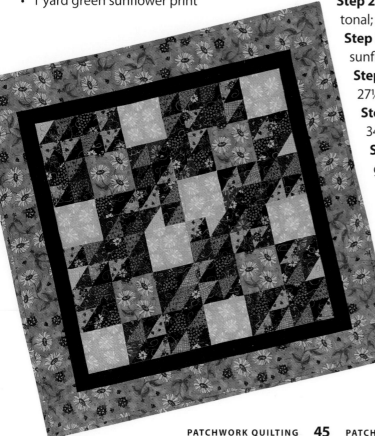

Figure 1; press seams to one side. Repeat to make 96 A units.

Step 3. Join two A units as shown in Figure 2; press seam in one direction. Repeat to make two joined units. Join these units with pressed seams in opposite directions to complete one A-A unit as shown in Figure 3; press seam in one direction. Repeat to make 24 A-A units.

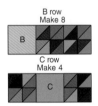

Figure 2   **Figure 3**

Step 4. Join a B square with two A-A units to make a B row as shown in Figure 4; press seams toward B. Repeat to make eight B rows.

B row
Make 8

C row
Make 4

Figure 4

Step 5. Sew a C square between two A-A units to make a C row, again referring to Figure 4; press seams toward C. Repeat to make four C rows.

Step 6. Join two B rows and one C row to complete one Sunflower block referring to the block drawing; repeat to make four blocks. Press seams toward B rows in two blocks and toward the C row in two blocks.

Completing the Quilt

Step 1. Join two blocks to make a row referring to the Placement Diagram for positioning of blocks; press seams in one direction. Repeat for a second row, pressing the seam in the opposite direction.

Step 2. Join the rows, again referring to the Placement Diagram for positioning; press seam in one direction.

Step 3. Sew a D strip to opposite sides and E strips to the top and bottom of the pieced centre; press seams toward D and E strips.

Step 4. Sew an F strip to opposite sides and G strips to the top and bottom of the pieced centre; press seams toward F and G strips to complete the pieced top.

Finishing Your Quilt

Step 1. Sandwich the batting between the completed top and prepared backing; pin or baste layers together to hold. ***Note:*** *If using basting spray to hold layers together, refer to instructions on the product container for use.*

Step 2. Quilt as desired by hand or machine; remove pins or basting. Trim excess backing and batting even with quilt top.

Step 3. Join binding strips on short ends to make one long strip. Fold the strip in half along length with wrong sides together; press.

Step 4. Sew binding to quilt edges, mitring corners and overlapping ends. Fold binding to the back side and stitch in place to finish. ✦

Sunflower Lane
Placement Diagram 34" x 34"

Which Way Home?

Uneven Flying Geese find their way across this table runner.

BY CHRISTINE SCHULTZ

Project Specifications
Skill Level: Intermediate
Runner Size: 58¼" x 16¼"

Materials
- Random scraps of light and dark fabrics
- ⅔ yard border and binding fabric
- 2 border stripe fabric strips 1½" x 48" (H)
- 1 border stripe fabric strip 1¾" x 55" (I)
- Backing 64" x 22"
- Batting 64" x 22"
- Neutral colour all-purpose thread
- Quilting thread

Instructions
Step 1. Prepare foundation copies as directed on pattern.
Step 2. Cut (10) 2½" x 2½" D squares, one 2½" x 4½" E rectangle, one 2½" x 1½" F rectangle and one 2½" x 6½" G rectangle light scraps.
Step 3. Using random scraps of dark for A and light for B and C, make 13 complete Flying Geese strips using paper foundation patterns, beginning at one end of the strip and continuing the piecing sequence in numerical order referring to Figure 1.

Figure 1

Step 4. Press finished pieced strips without steam and trim to outer cutting line. Do not remove paper.
Step 5. Referring to Figure 2, join four pairs of pieced Flying Geese strips together on the short

ends to make four 26-unit strips. Remove four geese units from one end of one strip to make a 22-unit strip.

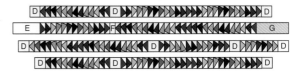

Figure 2

Step 6. Remove six geese units from one 13-unit strip to make a seven-unit strip.
Step 7. Join the units with D, E, F and G to make rows as shown in Figure 2.
Step 8. Fold each row, and each H and I strip, and crease to mark the centres. Align centres of rows, and H and I strips as shown in Figure 3; pin and stitch. **Note:** *Adjust strips as necessary to align Flying Geese units across the width of the runner, again referring to Figure 3. The ends of the strips will be staggered. Press seams toward H and I strips.*

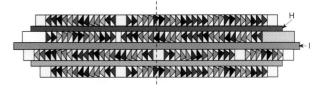

Figure 3

Step 9. Trim ends of pieced runner top by aligning the 45-degree diagonal line of a rotary ruler with the middle of the centre border strip and the two adjacent sides of the ruler at least ½" beyond the outer side of the last goose in each pieced strip as shown in Figure 4; trim to make angled ends.

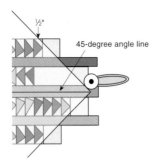

Figure 4

Step 10. Cut two 3" by fabric width J strips and four 3" x 14" K strips from border fabric.

Step 11. Centre and sew a J strip to opposite long sides of the pieced centre, stopping stitching at the end of the seam allowance and leaving strip extending on each end as shown in Figure 5; press seams toward J. Repeat with K strips on each end referring to Figure 6.

Figure 5

Figure 6

Step 12. Mitre corners at end points as shown in Figure 7; trim mitred seams to ¼" and press open.

Stitch angled corners at side edges as shown in Figure 8; trim angled seams to ¼" and press open.

Figure 7

Figure 8

Step 13. Remove paper foundations.

Step 14. Sandwich the batting between the completed top and prepared backing; pin or baste layers together to hold.

Step 15. Hand- or machine-quilt as desired. When quilting is complete, trim batting and backing even with top; remove pins or basting. **Note:** *The quilting design used on the sample is marked on the foundation pattern.*

Step 16. Cut six 1¼" by fabric width strips from binding fabric. Join strips on short ends to make one long strip. Fold one long edge under ¼"; press.

Step 17. Sew binding to quilt edges, mitring corners and overlapping ends. Fold binding to the backside and hand-stitch in place to finish. ✦

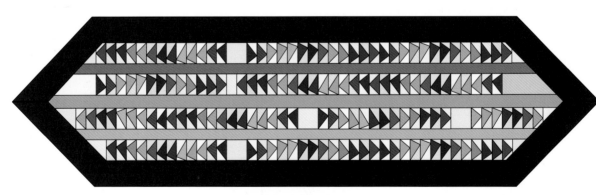

Which Way Home?
Placement Diagram 58¼" x 16¼"

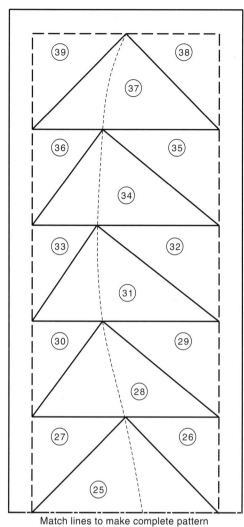

Match lines to make complete pattern

Flying Geese Foundation
Make 13 photocopies

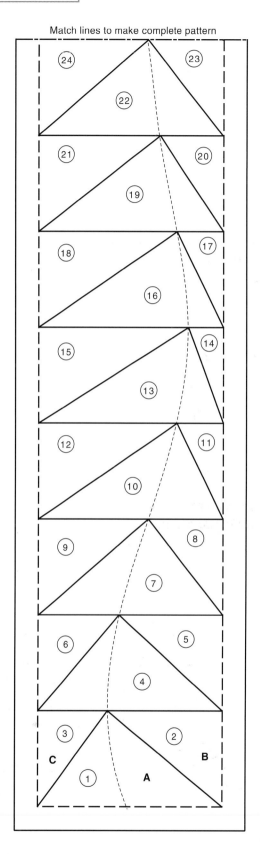

Match lines to make complete pattern

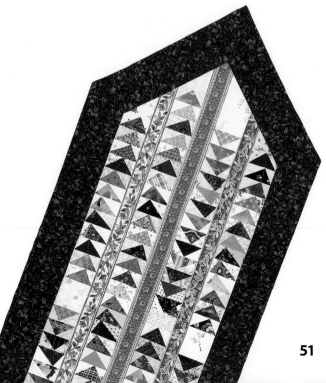

Denim Table Runner

Use up lots of denim scraps from your old jeans in this small table runner.

BY CONNIE KAUFFMAN

Project Specifications
Skill Level: Intermediate
Quilt Size: 26" x 14"

Materials
- 7" x 7" square denim for centre
- ¼ yard total denim scraps
- ¼ yard total indigo print scraps
- Backing 32" x 20"
- Batting 32" x 20"
- Matching all-purpose thread
- Quilting thread

Instructions
Step 1. Prepare templates using pattern pieces given; cut as directed on each piece.
Step 2. Lay out the pieces on a flat surface and stitch together aligning one end of each piece to make a straight edge in the following order, referring to Figure 1: A denim, B indigo, C denim, D indigo, D denim, D indigo, E denim, E indigo and E denim. Press seams in one direction. Repeat for two units.

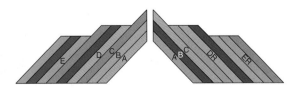

Figure 1

Step 3. Repeat with the remaining pieces in the following order, again referring to Figure 1: A indigo, B denim, C indigo, DR denim, DR indigo, DR

denim, ER indigo, ER denim and ER indigo. Press seams in opposite direction from previously pieced units. Repeat for two units.
Step 4. Join two units as shown in Figure 2, stopping stitching ¼" from the inside edge as shown in Figure 3; press seam open. Repeat with remaining two units.

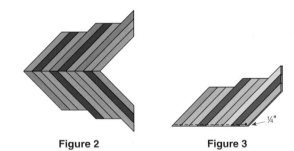

Figure 2   **Figure 3**

Step 5. Sew one side of the F square to the inside edge of one pieced unit, beginning and ending stitching at the ¼" seam as shown in Figure 4; stop and cut thread. Turn the piece and sew the adjacent side of the F square to the adjacent edge of the pieced unit in the same manner. Press seam away from F.

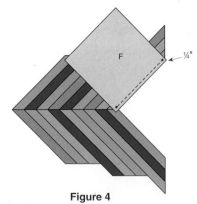

Figure 4

Step 6. Sew the remaining pieced unit to the F square in the same manner; press seams away from F.

Step 7. Fold the pieced unit right sides together down the centre of F as shown in Figure 5; stitch the edge seams from F to the outside as shown in Figure 6. Press seams open.

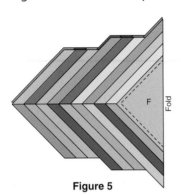

Figure 5

Figure 6

Step 8. Lay the batting piece on a flat surface with the backing piece right side up. Pin the completed runner top right sides together with the backing.

Step 9. Sew all around the outside edge, leaving a 4" opening along one end; trim batting and backing even with runner top, clip corners and inside corner seams and turn right side out through opening.

Step 10. Turn edge of opening to the inside; press the entire top flat. Hand-stitch the opening closed.

Step 11. Machine-quilt in the ditch of seams and in the centre of F using a fancy quilting design to finish. ✦

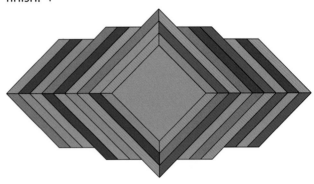

Denim Table Runner
Placement Diagram 26" x 14"

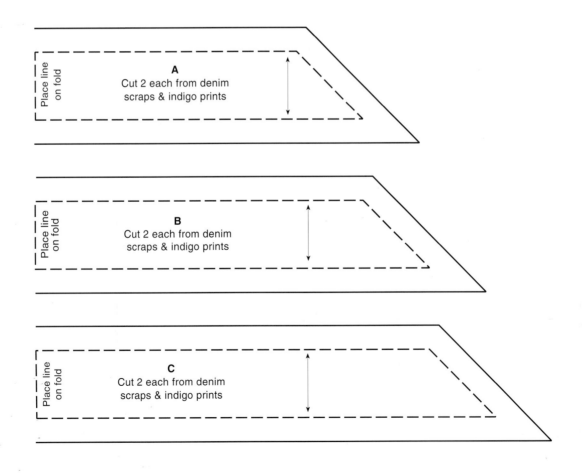

A
Cut 2 each from denim
scraps & indigo prints

Place line on fold

B
Cut 2 each from denim
scraps & indigo prints

Place line on fold

C
Cut 2 each from denim
scraps & indigo prints

Place line on fold

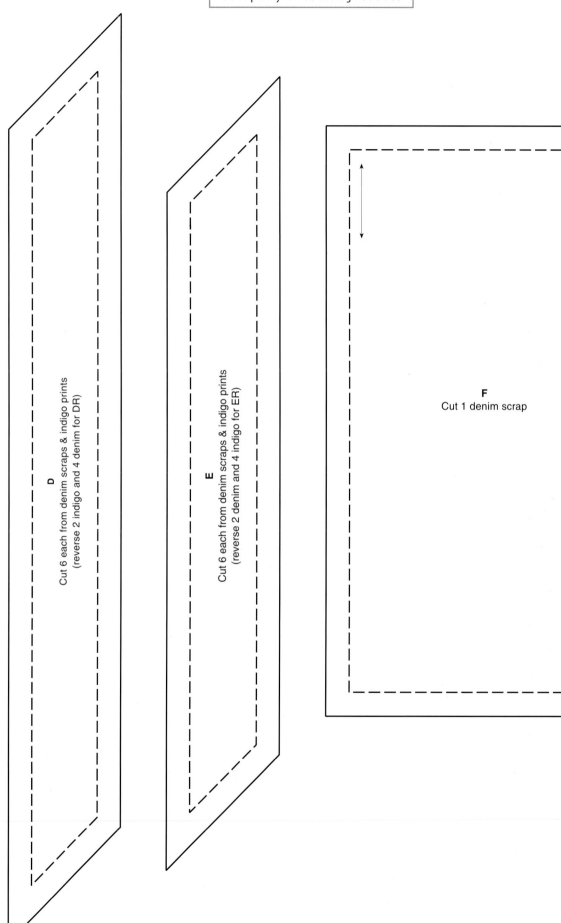

D
Cut 6 each from denim scraps & indigo prints
(reverse 2 indigo and 4 denim for DR)

E
Cut 6 each from denim scraps & indigo prints
(reverse 2 denim and 4 indigo for ER)

F
Cut 1 denim scrap

Place line on fold

Teddy Bear Quilt & Tote

Make this fringed baby quilt with matching tote using soft flannels or homespuns.

BY PEARL LOUISE KRUSH

Project Note

The quilt will fold up and fit nicely inside the tote bag for easy transportation.

Teddy Bear Quilt

Project Specifications

Skill Level: Beginner
Quilt Size: 32" x 32"

Materials

- 6" x 6" piece brown felt
- 8 fat quarters different plaids or prints of homespun or flannel
- 1 fat quarter light brown flannel
- 1 yard cotton batting
- 1¼ yards backing flannel or homespun
- All-purpose thread to match fabrics
- Light brown 6-strand embroidery floss

Instructions

Step 1. Cut two 10" x 10" squares from each plaid or print of homespun or flannel fat quarter.

Step 2. Cut sixteen 10" x 10" squares from backing flannel or homespun.

Step 3. Cut sixteen 8" x 8" squares cotton batting.

Step 4. Centre and sandwich an 8" x 8" square of batting between a 10" x 10" square of plaid or print and a backing square.

Step 5. Using a water-erasable marker or pencil, draw diagonal lines from corner to corner of each layered

Figure 1

square to make an X starting 1" from edge as shown in Figure 1.

Step 6. Stitch on marked lines on each layered unit, securing beginning and ending stitches.

Step 7. Arrange the squares in rows of four squares each, positioning squares with colours in a pleasing arrangement.

Step 8. Join the squares in rows with wrong sides together using a 1" seam allowance as shown in Figure 2; repeat for four rows. Press flat on the wrong side.

Figure 2

Step 9. Join rows with wrong sides together using a 1" seam; press flat on the wrong side.

Note: *The raw seam allowances will be on the right side of the quilt.*

Step 10. Prepare patterns for large bear pieces using patterns given; cut as directed on each piece.

Step 11. Layer two ear pieces with wrong sides together; stitch around curved sides using a ½" seam allowance. Sew the ears to two top angled edges of the head piece with wrong sides together using a ½" seam allowance.

Step 12. Centre and pin the head/ear shape to the stitched quilt top referring to the Placement Diagram for positioning; mark around outside of shapes on quilt using the water-erasable marker or pencil. Remove head/ear shape; trim seam allowances of quilt-top seams inside traced shape to ⅛."

Step 13. Pin the head/ear shape in place again; sew to the quilt top ½" from edge of shapes.

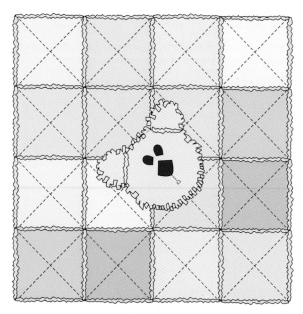

Teddy Bear Quilt
Placement Diagram
32" x 32"

Step 14. Stitch around outside of quilt 1" from edge. Clip the outer edge and each seam to within ⅛" of the stitched line every scant ¼." Repeat on head/ear shape seams and outer edge.

Step 15. Wash and dry the quilt to make edges fringe; remove all loose threads.

Step 16. Using 2 strands of brown embroidery floss, blanket-stitch the eyes and nose in place on the head/ear shape. Chain-stitch a mouth using drawing given to finish.

Teddy Bear Tote

Project Specifications
Skill Level: Beginner
Tote Size: 8" x 8" x 2"

Materials
- Scrap brown felt
- 1 fat quarter multicoloured plaid homespun or flannel
- 1 fat quarter yellow plaid homespun or flannel
- 1 fat quarter pink plaid homespun or flannel
- 1 fat quarter blue plaid homespun or flannel
- ½ yard cotton batting
- All-purpose thread to match fabrics
- Light brown 6-strand embroidery floss

Instructions
Step 1. Cut two 10" x 10" squares and three 4" x 10" rectangles each multicoloured plaid and yellow plaid homespun or flannel.

Step 2. Cut one 5" x 22" strip pink plaid homespun or flannel.

Step 3. Cut two 8" x 8" squares, three 2" x 8" rectangles and one 2" x 21" strip cotton batting.

Step 4. Centre and sandwich the 8" x 8" batting square between one multicoloured plaid and one yellow plaid 10" x 10" square; repeat with second set of squares.

Step 5. Mark and stitch each layered square referring to Steps 5 and 6 for Teddy Bear Quilt.

Step 6. Centre and layer the 2" x 8" batting rectangles with the 4" x 10" fabric rectangles to make gusset pieces.

Step 7. Mark and stitch each layered gusset piece as in Step 5.

Step 8. Prepare patterns for small bear pieces using patterns given; cut as directed on each piece.

Step 9. Layer two ear pieces with wrong sides together; stitch around curved sides using a ½" seam allowance. Sew the ears to two top angled edges of the head piece with wrong sides together using a ½" seam allowance.

Step 10. Centre and pin the head/ear shape on one stitched-and-layered square. Stitch in place, leaving a ½" seam allowance all around.

Step 11. Join the three gusset pieces on short ends with yellow sides together using a 1" seam allowance.

Step 12. Pin the gusset strip around three sides of the appliquéd square with yellow sides together as shown in Figure 3; stitch using a 1" seam allowance. Repeat with the remaining layered square. Stitch around top of bag 1" from outer edge.

Figure 3

Step 13. Press under ¼" along long edges and each end of the 5" x 22" strip pink plaid. Centre the 2" x 21" strip batting on the wrong side of the strip;

fold sides over batting, overlapping as needed. Stitch along overlapped seam and ¼" from all edges as shown in Figure 4 to complete strap.

Figure 4

Step 14. Pin and stitch strap ends to top inside edges of the stitched bag; stitch in place.
Step 15. Clip outside edge and each seam to within ⅛" of the stitched line every scant ¼." Repeat on bear shape seams and outer edge.
Step 16. Wash and dry the bag to make edges fringe; remove all loose threads.

Step 17. Using 2 strands of light brown embroidery floss, blanket-stitch the eyes and nose in place on the bear/ear shape. Chain-stitch a mouth using drawing given to finish. ◆

Teddy Bear Tote
Placement Diagram
8" x 8" x 2"

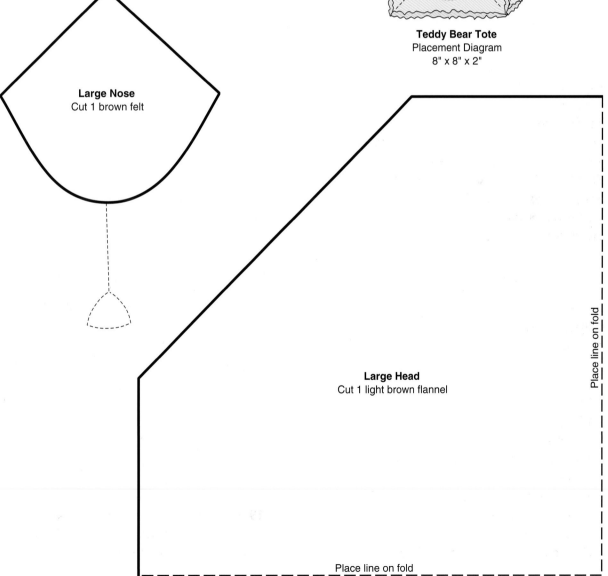

Large Nose
Cut 1 brown felt

Large Head
Cut 1 light brown flannel

Place line on fold

Place line on fold

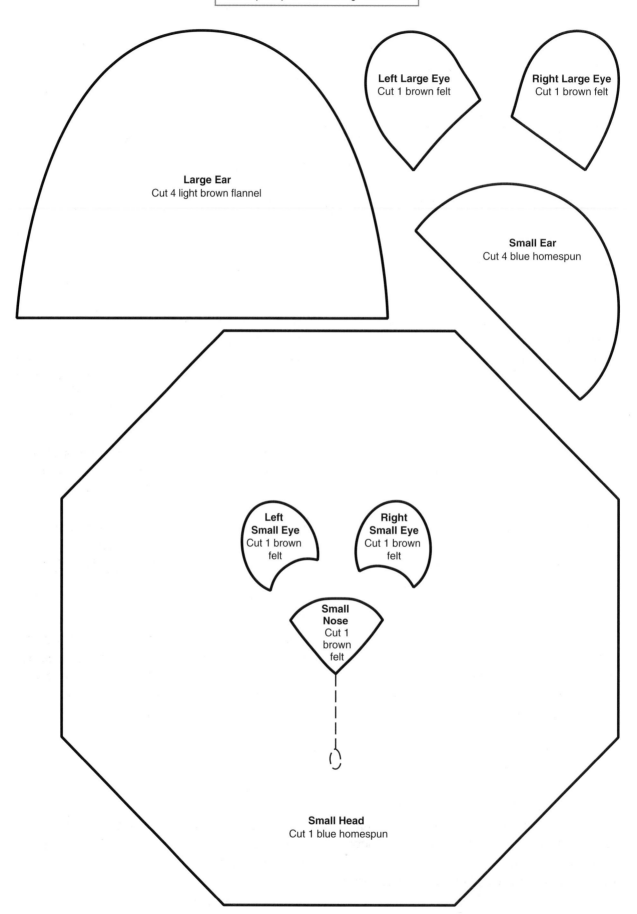

Large Ear
Cut 4 light brown flannel

Left Large Eye
Cut 1 brown felt

Right Large Eye
Cut 1 brown felt

Small Ear
Cut 4 blue homespun

**Left
Small Eye**
Cut 1 brown
felt

**Right
Small Eye**
Cut 1 brown
felt

**Small
Nose**
Cut 1
brown
felt

Small Head
Cut 1 blue homespun

Grandma's Joy

Two easy blocks and flannel prints stitch up in a weekend, making this lap-size quilt to keep your little one warm.

DESIGN BY JULIE WEAVER

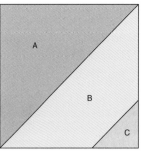

Edge
6" x 6" Block
Make 24

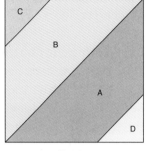

Centre
6" x 6" Block
Make 24

Project Specifications
Skill Level: Beginner
Quilt Size: 50" x 62"
Block Size: 6" x 6"
Number of Blocks: 48

Materials
All fabrics are flannel
- 1/3 yard blue dot
- 1 yard yellow print
- 1¼ yards yellow dot
- 1¾ yards blue print
- Backing 56" x 68"
- Batting 56" x 68"
- All-purpose thread to match fabrics
- Quilting thread

Instructions
Cutting
Step 1. Cut four 6⅞" by fabric width strips each blue (A) and yellow (B) prints; subcut strips into (24) 6⅞" squares each fabric.

Step 2. Cut five 5½" by fabric width strips blue print. Join strips on short ends to make one long strip; press seams open. Subcut strip into two 52½" G strips and two 40½" H strips.

Step 3. Cut three 2½" by fabric width strips blue dot; subcut strips into (48) 2½" C squares. Draw a diagonal line from corner to corner on the wrong side of each square.

Step 4. Cut two 2½" by fabric width strips yellow dot; subcut strips into (24) 2½" D squares. Draw a diagonal line from corner to corner on the wrong side of each square.

Step 5. Cut five 2½" by fabric width strips yellow dot. Join strips on short ends to make one long strip; press seams open. Subcut strip into two 48½" E strips and two 40½" F strips.

Step 6. Cut one 5½" by fabric width strip yellow dot; subcut strip into four 5½" I squares.

Step 7. Cut six 2½" by fabric width strips yellow dot for binding.

Completing the A-B Units
Step 1. Draw a diagonal line on the wrong side of each A square. Place a B square right sides together with an A square and stitch ¼" on each side of the marked line as shown in Figure 1. Repeat for all A and B squares.

Figure 1   **Figure 2**

Step 2. Cut each stitched unit apart on the marked lines to make A-B units as shown in Figure 2; press seams toward A.

Completing the Edge Blocks

Step 1. Place a C square right sides together on the corner of B and stitch on the marked line as shown in Figure 3.

Figure 3

Step 2. Trim seam allowance to ¼" and press C to the right side to complete one Edge block, again referring to Figure 3; repeat to make 24 Edge blocks.

Completing the Centre Blocks

Step 1. Repeat Steps 1 and 2 for Completing the Edge Blocks with remaining A-B units and C squares.
Step 2. Place a D square right sides together on the corner of A and stitch on the marked line as shown in Figure 4.

Figure 4

Step 3. Trim seam allowance to ¼" and press D to the right side to complete one Centre block, again referring to Figure 4; repeat to make 24 Centre blocks.

Completing the Quilt

Step 1. Arrange six Edge blocks to make an X row as shown in Figure 5; press seams in one direction. Repeat to make two X rows.

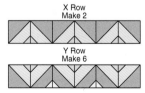

Figure 5

Step 2. Join two Edge blocks with four Centre blocks to make a Y row, again referring to Figure 5; press seams in the opposite direction from the X rows. Repeat to make six Y rows.
Step 3. Join the X and Y rows referring to the Placement Diagram for positioning of rows; press seams in one direction.
Step 4. Sew an E strip to opposite long sides and F strips to the top and bottom of the pieced centre; press seams toward E and F strips.
Step 5. Sew a G strip to opposite long sides of the pieced centre; press seams toward G strips.
Step 6. Sew an I square to each end of each H strip; press seams toward H strips.
Step 7. Sew an H-I strip to the top and bottom of the pieced centre to complete the pieced top; press seams toward the H-I strips.
Step 8. Complete the quilt referring to General Instructions. ◆

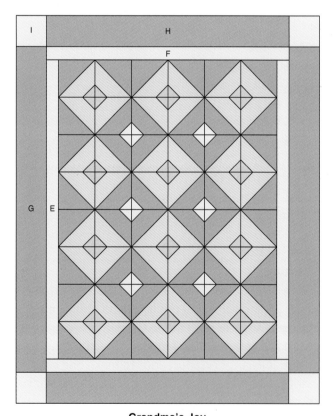

Grandma's Joy
Placement Diagram
50" x 62"

Teddy-Go-Round

Make a play-on-the-floor quilt for a small child who will be happy to have friendly teddy bears peering up at him.

BY SUE HARVEY

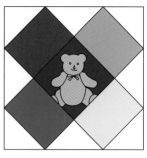

Bear's Fancy
12" x 12" Block

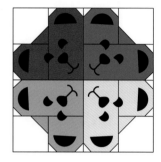

Teddy-Go-Round
12" x 12" Block

Project Specifications
Skill Level: Intermediate
Quilt Size: 44½" x 44½"
Block Size: 12" x 12"
Number of Blocks: 9

Materials
• 4 fat quarters bright-coloured prints
• 1 fat quarter black print
• ¾ yard white print
• 1½ yards bear print
• Batting 49" x 49"
• Backing 49" x 49"
• All-purpose thread to match fabrics
• Black machine-embroidery thread
• ¼ yard fusible transfer web
• 1 yard fabric stabilizer
• Basting spray

Instructions
Step 1. Cut two strips 4¾" x 36½" across width of bear print; cut two strips 4¾" x 36½" along length of bear print. Set aside for borders. **Note:** *For a non-directional print, cut all four strips across the width of the fabric.*

Step 2. Cut four squares bear print 5½" x 5½" for K. **Note:** *For a directional print, cut on the fabric diagonal to keep print upright in blocks.*

Step 3. Cut three strips white print 1¼" by fabric width; subcut each strip into 1¼" square segments for C. You will need 80 C squares.

Step 4. Cut two strips white print 3½" by fabric width; subcut each strip into 3½" square segments for D. You will need 20 D squares.

Step 5. Cut one strip white print 4⅜" by fabric width; subcut into eight 4⅜" square segments. Cut each square on one diagonal to make H triangles; you will need 16 H triangles.

Step 6. Cut one strip white print 6¼" by fabric width; subcut into four 6¼" square segments. Cut each square on both diagonals to make J triangles; you will need 16 J triangles.

Step 7. From each bright fat quarter, cut the following strips: one 6½" x 18"—subcut into five 3½" segments for A; one 3½" x 18"—subcut into five 3½" squares for B; one 1¾" x 18"—subcut into five 1¾" squares for E; and one 5½" x 18" —subcut into four 4" segments for G.

Step 8. Mark a diagonal line from corner to corner on the wrong side of each C and E square.

Step 9. To piece one teddy unit, place a C square right sides together on two adjacent corners of A as shown in Figure 1; stitch on the marked line, trim seam allowance to ¼" and press C open as shown in Figure 2. Repeat on a same-colour B as shown in Figure 3.

Figure 1

Figure 2

Figure 3

Step 10. Place a same-colour E on one corner of D; stitch, trim and press E open as shown in Figure 4.

Figure 4

Step 11. Sew B-C to D-E as shown in Figure 5; add A-C to complete one teddy unit, again referring to Figure 5. Repeat to make four teddy units of each colour.

Figure 5

Step 12. Trace large teddy eye, ear and nose pieces on the paper side of the fusible transfer web referring to the patterns for number to trace of each; fuse to the wrong side of the black print.

Step 13. Cut out each piece on the traced line; remove paper backing.

Step 14. Fuse one nose, two eye and two ear pieces to each teddy unit referring to the block drawing for positioning; mark the mouth shape given below each nose piece. Pin a piece of fabric stabilizer on the wrong side of each teddy unit.

Step 15. Using black machine-embroidery thread in the top of the machine and all-purpose thread in the bobbin, and a medium-width zigzag stitch, machine-stitch around each fused shape and along the marked mouth lines; remove fabric stabilizer.

Step 16. Join one teddy unit of each colour to complete one Teddy-Go-Round block referring to the block drawing for positioning of units; repeat for five blocks.

Step 17. To piece one Bear's Fancy block, sew J to opposite ends of one bright G as shown in Figure 6; add H to one long side, again referring to Figure 6. Repeat with different-colour G.

Figure 6

Step 18. Sew a G of the remaining two colours to opposite sides of K as shown in Figure 7; add H to the G ends of the pieced unit, again referring to Figure 7.

Figure 7

Step 19. Join the pieced units to complete one Bear's Fancy block referring to the block drawing for positioning; repeat for four blocks.

Step 20. Join the blocks in three rows of three blocks each as shown in Figure 8; join the rows to complete the pieced centre.

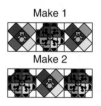

Figure 8

Step 21. From each bright fat quarter, cut the following: one 2" x 18" strip—subcut into one 3½" segment for A, one 2" square for B and one 1¼" x 1¼" square for E.

Step 22. From white print, cut the following: 16 squares ⅞" x ⅞" for C, four squares 2" x 2" for D and eight squares 3" x 3" for F. Cut each F square in half on one diagonal to make 16 F triangles.

Step 23. Piece one small teddy unit of each colour referring to steps 8–11. Sew an F triangle to each side of the teddy units to complete a corner unit.

Step 24. Mark the small teddy mouth, nose, eye and ear shapes on each unit using the pattern given; pin a piece of fabric stabilizer on the wrong side of each corner unit.

Step 25. Using black machine-embroidery thread in the top of the machine and all-purpose thread in the bobbin, machine satin-stitch each shape; remove fabric stabilizer.

Step 26. Sew a fabric-length strip cut in Step 1 to opposite sides of the pieced centre; press seams toward strips.

Step 27. Sew a corner unit to opposite ends of each remaining bear print strip; sew a strip to the top and bottom of the pieced centre to complete the top. Press seams toward strips.

Step 28. Apply basting spray to one side of the batting piece; place on the wrong side of the prepared backing piece. Repeat with completed top.

Step 29. Quilt as desired. ***Note:*** *The sample shown was professionally machine-quilted in an allover pattern.*

Step 30. Prepare 5½ yards self-made bear print binding and apply referring to the General Instructions. ◆

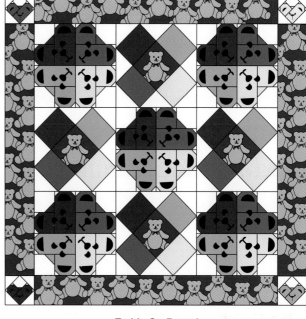

Teddy-Go-Round
Placement Diagram
44¹⁄₂" x 44¹⁄₂"

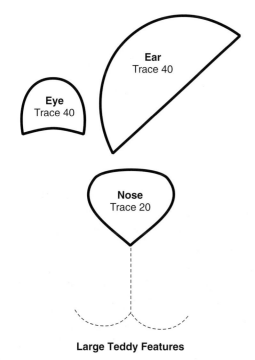

Ear
Trace 40

Eye
Trace 40

Nose
Trace 20

Large Teddy Features

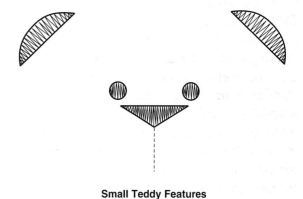

Small Teddy Features

Come Rain or Shine

Rainy days never looked so cheerful as they do on this colourful pieced-and-appliquéd quilt.

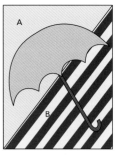

Umbrella Fun
7" x 9" Block
Make 25

BY CHERYL ADAM FOR WESTMINSTER FIBERS

Project Specifications
Skill Level: Beginner
Quilt Size: 52" x 62"
Block Size: 7" x 9"
Number of Blocks: 25

Materials
- 25 (4" x 8") rectangles assorted bright prints
- 13 (14" x 14") B squares assorted stripes
- 13 (7¾" x 10") A rectangles assorted prints
- ⅛ yard brown solid
- ½ yard blue/green stripe
- 1⅔ yards purple print stripe
- 1⅔ yards yellow print stripe
- 1⅔ yards green solid
- Backing 58" x 68"
- Batting 58" x 68"
- Neutral colour all-purpose thread
- Quilting thread
- 2⅛ yards fusible web

Instructions
Cutting
Step 1. Trace 25 umbrella shapes onto the paper side of the fusible web; cut out shapes, leaving a margin around each one.
Step 2. Fuse a paper umbrella shape to the wrong side of each 4" x 8" bright-print rectangle; cut out shapes on traced lines. Remove paper backing.
Step 3. Bond fusible web to the wrong side of the brown solid; trace 25 handle shapes onto the

paper side of the fused fabric. Cut out shapes on traced lines; remove paper backing.
Step 4. Cut each 7¾" x 10" print A rectangle in half on one diagonal as shown in Figure 1 to make A triangles; discard one triangle.

Figure 1

Step 5. Pair up two A triangles with each 14" x 14" stripe B square; place one A triangle right side up on the B square, aligning the diagonal straight edge of A with a stripe on the square as shown in Figure 2. Repeat with the second A on the remaining half of B, again referring to Figure 2.

Figure 2

Step 6. Pin edges of A to secure on the square; cut around the A triangles to make two B stripe triangles as shown in Figure 3; repeat to make 25 A-B pairs.

Figure 3

Step 7. Cut six 2" x 54½" C strips along the length of the green solid.

Step 8. Cut two 7½" by remaining fabric width strips green solid; subcut strips into (30) 2" D strips.

Step 9. Cut one 4½" x 54½" E strip along the length of the purple print stripe; repeat with the yellow print stripe to cut an F strip.

Step 10. Cut two 4½" by remaining fabric width strips purple print stripe. Join strips on short ends to make one long strip; press seam open. Subcut strip into one 52½" G strip.

Step 11. Repeat Step 10 with the yellow print stripe to make one H strip.

Step 12. Cut six 2¼" by fabric width strips blue/green stripe for binding.

Completing the Blocks

Step 1. Sew A to B along the diagonal as shown in Figure 4; open and press seam toward A to complete an A-B unit. Repeat to make 25 A-B units.

Figure 4

Step 2. Fold each A-B unit in half horizontally and vertically and crease to mark the centre.

Step 3. Centre an umbrella shape on each A-B unit, tucking the handle shape under the umbrella shape as shown on the pattern for placement and referring to the block drawing; fuse in place to complete the Umbrella blocks.

Completing the Quilt

Step 1. Join five Umbrella blocks with six D pieces to make a vertical row as shown in Figure 5; press seams toward D. Repeat to make five vertical rows.

Figure 5

Step 2. Join the vertical rows with the C strips to complete the pieced centre; press seams toward C strips.

Step 3. Sew the E strip to the right-side edge and the F strip to the left-side edge of the pieced centre; press seams toward E and F strips.

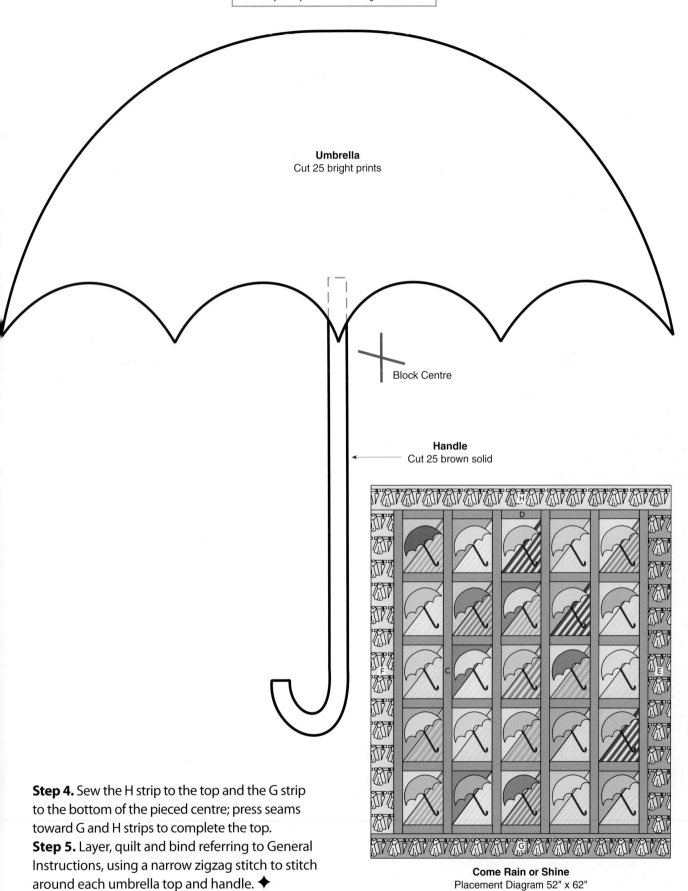

Umbrella
Cut 25 bright prints

Block Centre

Handle
Cut 25 brown solid

Come Rain or Shine
Placement Diagram 52" x 62"

Step 4. Sew the H strip to the top and the G strip to the bottom of the pieced centre; press seams toward G and H strips to complete the top.
Step 5. Layer, quilt and bind referring to General Instructions, using a narrow zigzag stitch to stitch around each umbrella top and handle. ✦

Rag-Seam Quilt & Pillow

Cut up those old denim skirts and jumpers to use in the blocks of this quick-to-stitch quilt with matching pillow.

BY PEARL LOUISE KRUSH

Rag-Seam Quilt

Project Specifications
Skill Level: Beginner
Quilt Size: 63" x 74"
Block Size: 11" x 11"
Number of Blocks: 30

Materials
- 15 (12" x 12") squares recycled denim (B)
- 8 (5" x 5") squares recycled denim (F)
- 1¾ yards 58"–60"-wide cream-red-blue stripe ticking
- 2 yards red twill
- 3½ yards blue plaid flannel
- 4 yards thin cotton batting
- All-purpose thread to match fabrics

Instructions
Note: Prewash and press all fabrics before cutting; use a ½" seam allowance throughout.

Step 1. Cut (15) 12" x 12" squares each cream-red-blue stripe ticking for A.

Step 2. Cut (30) 12" x 12" squares blue plaid flannel for C backing pieces.

Step 3. Cut (30) 11" x 11" squares thin cotton batting.

Step 4. Centre and sandwich a batting square between A and C squares with right sides out; repeat with B and C squares.

Step 5. Machine-stitch an X through the centre of each sandwiched unit as shown in Figure 1.

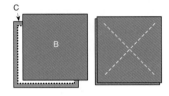

Figure 1

Step 6. Arrange the stitched units in six rows of five units each referring to the Placement Diagram for positioning of units.

Step 7. Place two units with the C backing pieces together; stitch using a ½" seam allowance. Continue stitching units to complete rows.

Step 8. Join the rows as in step 7.

Step 9. Cut (12) 5" by fabric width strips red twill. Join strips on short ends to make one long strip. Subcut the strip into four 56" D strips and four 67" E strips.

Step 10. Cut and piece together two 4" x 55" and two 4" x 66" batting strips.

Step 11. Centre and sandwich a 4" x 55" batting strip between two D strips; repeat with the 4" x 66" batting strips and the E strips.

Step 12. Draw a V-shaped quilting pattern onto the top layer of the strips as shown in Figure 2; sew on the drawn lines to hold the strips together.

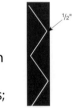

Figure 2

Step 13. Cut four 4" x 4" batting squares; centre and sandwich the batting between two 5" x 5" denim F squares; stitch from corner to corner to make an X in the square. Repeat for four stitched corner units.

Step 14. Sew the quilted E strips to opposite long sides of the pieced centre as in step 7. Sew an F unit to each end of the D strips and sew to the top and bottom of the pieced centre as in step 7.

Step 15. Cut six 2" by fabric width strips cream-red-blue stripe ticking. Join strips on short ends to make one long strip for binding; press over ¼" on one long edge.

Step 16. Pin binding strip with right sides together and raw edges aligned to the wrong side of the stitched top; stitch using a ½" seam allowance, mitring corners and overlapping ends.

Step 17. Fold the binding ½" to the right side of the quilt; machine-stitch close to the edge of the binding on the right side to hold in place as shown in Figure 3.

Figure 3

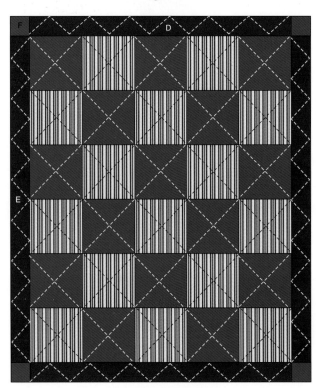

Rag-Seam Quilt
Placement Diagram
63" x 74"

Step 18. Clip all exposed seams almost to the stitched seam line, clipping ¼" apart as shown in Figure 4.

Figure 4

Step 19. Wash the quilt in a washing machine and dry in a dryer. Clean the filters in both washer and dryer to remove the loose threads and lint. Shake the quilt to remove any remaining threads.

Rag-Seam Pillow

Project Specifications
Skill Level: Beginner
Pillow Size: 16" x 16"

Materials
- 2 (7") G squares recycled denim
- 2 (12" x 17") H rectangles recycled denim
- 2 (7") I squares cream-red-blue stripe ticking
- 2 (3" x 13") J rectangles red twill
- 2 (3" x 17") K rectangles red twill
- 4 (6") squares thin cotton batting
- 2 rectangles each 2" x 12" and 2" x 16" thin cotton batting
- Neutral-colour all-purpose thread
- 1 (16") pillow form

Instructions
Note: All seams are sewn with wrong sides together using a ½" seam allowance throughout.

Step 1. Centre and pin the 6" batting squares to the wrong side of the G and I squares.

Step 2. Sew an X through the centres of the squares as in Figure 1 for quilt.

Figure 5

Step 3. Arrange the G and I squares in two rows of two squares each, referring to Figure 5; join squares in rows with batting sides together. Join the rows in the same manner.

Step 4. Centre and pin batting rectangles to J and K rectangles as in step 1; sew down the centre of each layered rectangle.

Step 5. Sew a layered J strip to opposite sides of the stitched centre as in step 3, keeping seams on the right side. Repeat on the remaining sides with the layered K strips.

Step 6. Fold and press one 17" edge of each H rectangle under ½;" repeat and stitch to hem. Repeat on the second H rectangle.

Step 7. Pin H rectangles wrong sides together with the stitched top, overlapping 4" on edges as shown in Figure 6; stitch all around the outside edges using a ½" seam allowance.

Step 8. Clip all seams every ¼" to the stitched seam line.

Step 9. Wash and dry pillow cover as for quilt. Insert pillow form to finish. ◆

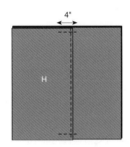

Figure 6

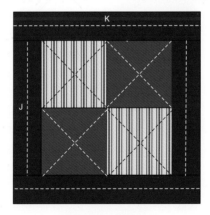

Rag-Seam Pillow
Placement Diagram
16" x 16"

Happy Birthday Banner

Make a birthday banner that will last through the years.

BY CHRISTINE BAKER & NELLIE HOLMES

Project Specifications
Skill Level: Beginner
Banner Size: 15" x 24½"

Materials
All fabrics are wool
- 20" x 32" cream for background and backing
- 10" x 12" cream for tabs and fringe
- 6 (4" x 5") rectangles various colours for number backgrounds
- Scraps up to 4" x 4" in bright colours for appliquéd numbers and shapes
- Assorted colours embroidery floss to match or contrast with appliqué shapes and to finish edges
- Black embroidery floss
- 1 yard freezer paper
- 6 (½") buttons for hats
- 2 (¾") buttons to attach removable numbers
- Basting spray
- 15" hanging dowel or quilt hanger

Instructions
Preparing & Cutting Wool
Step 1. If your wool is already felted, it is ready to use and requires no further preparation. If your wool is not felted, wash it in hot water with a small amount of detergent; rinse in cold water. Dry the wet wool in a hot dryer to make ready to use.
Step 2. Cut two 15" x 19" cream rectangles for background and backing.
Step 3. Cut four 1½" x 7" hanging tab strips from the 10" x 12" felted cream rectangle.

Preparing Appliqué Shapes
Step 1. Trace all appliqué shapes given onto the dull side of the freezer paper, leaving at least ¼" between the shapes; cut out shapes on the drawn lines.
Step 2. Place the freezer-paper templates shiny side down on the bright scraps.
Step 3. Place the fringe templates shiny side down on the remainder of the 10" x 12" cream rectangle.
Step 4. Using a warm iron, iron the freezer-paper templates to the wool.
Step 5. Cut out each shape along the edge of the freezer-paper template; peel the freezer-paper off the cut shapes.
Step 6. Referring to the Placement Diagram and colour photo of the project, pin, thread-baste or spray-baste pieces in place on one piece of cream background.
Step 7. Using 2 strands of matching or contrasting embroidery floss, blanket-stitch around the outside edges of each shape.

Blanket Stitch

Step 8. Using 3 strands of black embroidery floss, backstitch strings on the bottom of the

Backstitch

balloons and party hats using the dotted lines on the pattern page as guides for stitching.
Step 9. Sew three small buttons to each party hat and the two larger buttons 2" apart in the centre of the banner for attaching the number background rectangles.

Preparing the Fringe

Step 1. Centre and pin, thread-baste or spray-baste a circle to the centre of five fringe pieces.

Step 2. Blanket-stitch around each shape with 2 strands of embroidery floss to match each shape.

Step 3. Place each appliquéd fringe shape on a plain fringe shape.

Step 4. Select one colour of embroidery floss to finish edges of fringe pieces and banner. Using 2 strands of selected floss, blanket-stitch around the outside curved edges of each layered fringe shape to hold layers together.

Preparing Button-on Numbers

Step 1. Thread- or spray-baste the desired numbers onto the 4" x 5" coloured rectangles; blanket-stitch shapes in place using 2 strands of matching embroidery floss.

Step 2. Align the top edge of each number rectangle with buttons; mark and cut two buttonholes on the top corner of each.

Step 3. Blanket-stitch around each buttonhole and around outside edge of each rectangle using 2 strands of matching embroidery floss.

Completing the Banner

Step 1. Lay the 15" x 19" backing piece on a hard surface with the right side down; lay the appliquéd top rectangle on top of the backing piece right side up.

Step 2. Referring to Figure 1, arrange the fringe pieces along the bottom edge, leaving approximately ½" between each one. Slip each fringe between the backing and top layers approximately ½;" pin to hold.

Step 3. Check fringe alignment for even spacing; adjust, if necessary.

Step 4. Fold each of the hanging tabs in half to make four 1½" x 3½" tabs.

Figure 1

Step 5. Again referring to Figure 1, arrange the folded hanging tabs along the top edge of the banner, leaving approximately 2" between tabs referring to the Placement Diagram.

Step 6. Check hanging-tab alignment; adjust if necessary.

Step 7. Slip each hanging tab between the backing and top layers approximately ½;" pin to hold.

Step 8. Using 2 strands of selected floss, blanket-stitch around the outside edges through all layers, hiding knots and ends between layers.

Step 9. Hang on a 15" dowel or quilt hanger. ◆

Happy Birthday Banner
Placement Diagram 15" x 24½"

Trace 2

Trace 2

Trace 2

Trace 4

Trace 2

Trace 3

Balloon
Trace 3

Hat
Trace 2

Fringe
Trace 10

Circle
Trace 5

Ribbon
Trace 3

Nana's Cups & Saucers

Remember your grandmother with this cup-and-saucer–motif wall quilt and matching runner.

BY CATE TALLMAN-EVANS

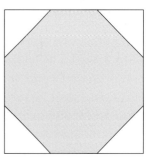

Saucer
7½" x 7½" Block
Make 24

Teacup
7½" x 7½" Block
Make 16

Broken Dishes
3¼" x 3¼" Block
Make 36

Project Specifications
Skill Level: Beginner
Quilt Size: 62½" x 62½"
Block Size: 7½" x 7½"
Number of Blocks: 40
Runner Size: Approximately 55" x 18½"
Block Size: 3¼" x 3¼"
Number of Blocks: 36

Materials
- 16 fat quarters assorted floral prints
- 8 fat quarters assorted cream tonals
- 3 yards green print
- Backing 68" x 68" and 61" x 24"
- Batting 68" x 68" and 61" x 24"
- Neutral-colour and cream all-purpose thread
- Quilting thread
- Clear monofilament
- 2 yards 12"-wide lightweight double-sided fusible web

Instructions
Cutting
Step 1. Referring to Figure 1, cut two 8" x 8" A squares and (15) 3" x 3" E squares from each cream tonal fat quarter.

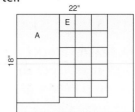

Figure 1

Step 2. Fold each A square horizontally and vertically, and crease to mark the centres.

Step 3. Mark a line diagonally from corner to corner on the wrong side of each E square; set aside 24 squares for runner.

Step 4. Trace 16 teacup shapes onto the paper side of the double-sided fusible web, leaving ½" between motifs.

Step 5. Cut out paper shapes, leaving a ¼" margin around each one.

Step 6. Referring to Figure 2, cut an 8" x 8" D square and two 3" x 3" D squares and fuse a teacup shape to the wrong side of each floral print fat quarter. Cut a second 8" x 8" D square from eight of the fabrics. Set aside smaller D squares for runner.

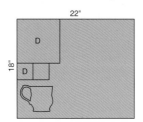

Figure 2

Step 7. Cut out teacup shapes on traced lines; remove paper backing.

Step 8. Cut four 4¼" by fabric width strips green print; subcut strips to make two 30½" B strips and two 38" C strips.

Step 9. Cut six 5½" by fabric width strips green print. Join strips on short ends to make one long strip; press seams open. Subcut strip into two 53" F strips and two 63" G strips.

Step 10. Cut one 19⅝" by fabric width strip green print; subcut strip into one 19⅝" H square, three 7" x 7" I squares and two 10⅛" x 10⅛" J squares. Cut the H square in half on both diagonals and the J squares in half on one diagonal to make four each H and J triangles.

Step 11. Cut (11) 2¼" by fabric width strips green print for binding.

Completing the Teacup Blocks

Step 1. Centre a teacup on an A square using the marked centre on the pattern and creased lines of A as a guide; fuse shape in place. Repeat for 16 teacup/A units.

Step 2. Using clear monofilament, stitch a straight line close to the edge all around each teacup shape as shown in Figure 3 to complete the 16 Teacup blocks.

Figure 3

Completing the Saucer Blocks

Step 1. Referring to Figure 4, place an E square right sides together on each corner of D and stitch on the marked line.

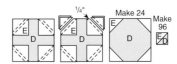

Figure 4

Step 2. Repeat stitching ⅜"–½" from stitched seam, again referring to Figure 4. Cut apart between stitching lines and press seam toward E to make one Saucer block and four D-E bonus units, again referring to Figure 4.

Step 3. Repeat Steps 1 and 2 to complete 24 Saucer blocks and 96 D-E bonus units.

Step 4. Trim the D-E bonus units to 2⅛" x 2⅛;" set aside for runner.

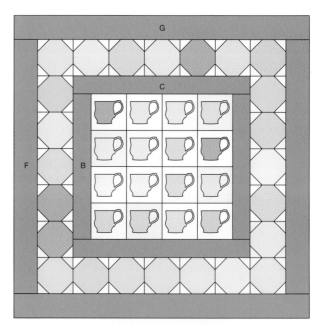

Nana's Cups & Saucers
Placement Diagram 62½" x 62½"

Completing the Quilt

Step 1. Join four Teacup blocks to make a row; press seams in one direction. Repeat for four rows, pressing seams in adjacent rows in opposite directions.

Step 2. Join the rows to complete the pieced centre; press seams in one direction.

Step 3. Sew B strips to opposite sides and C strips to the top and bottom of the completed centre; press seams toward B and C strips.

Step 4. Join five Saucer blocks to make a row; press seams in one direction. Repeat for two rows. Sew these rows to opposite sides of the quilt centre; press seams toward B and C strips.

Step 5. Join seven Saucer blocks to make the top row; press seams in one direction. Repeat for bottom row. Sew these rows to the top and bottom of the quilt centre; press seams toward B and C strips.

Step 6. Sew F strips to opposite sides and G strips to the top and bottom of the quilt centre to complete the top; press seams toward F and G strips.

Step 7. Layer, quilt and bind.

Completing the Broken Dishes Blocks

Step 1. Place a 3" x 3" D square right sides together with an E square; stitch ¼" on both sides of the marked line as shown in Figure 5. *Note: Use D and E squares cut in Steps 1 and 6 in the Cutting instructions.*

Step 2. Cut apart on the marked line and press units open to complete two D-E units, again referring to Figure 5; repeat for 48 D-E units. Trim each unit to 2⅛" x 2⅛" as for the D-E bonus units. Set aside remaining D squares for another use.

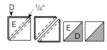

Figure 5   **Figure 6**

Step 3. To complete one Broken Dishes block, join two D-E units as shown in Figure 6; press seam in one direction. Repeat for two units.

Step 4. Join the two pieced units to complete one block referring to the block drawing; repeat for 36 blocks.

Completing the Runner

Step 1. Join two Broken Dishes blocks as shown in Figure 7; press seam in one direction. Repeat for two rows.

Figure 7   **Figure 8**

Step 2. Sew the two rows to opposite sides of an I square as shown in Figure 8; press seams toward I.

Step 3. Join four Broken Dishes blocks as shown in Figure 9; press seams in one direction. Repeat for two rows.

Figure 9

Step 4. Sew the two rows to the remaining sides of I to complete an I unit as shown in Figure 10; press seams toward I. Repeat for three I units.

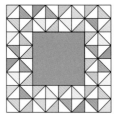

Figure 10

Step 5. Join the I units with H and J triangles in diagonal rows as shown in Figure 11; press seams toward H and J.

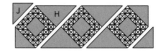

Figure 11

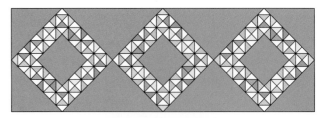

Broken Dishes Runner
Placement Diagram Approximately 55" x 18½"

Step 6. Join the rows to complete the runner top; press seams in one direction.

Step 7. Layer, quilt and bind referring to General Instructions. ◆

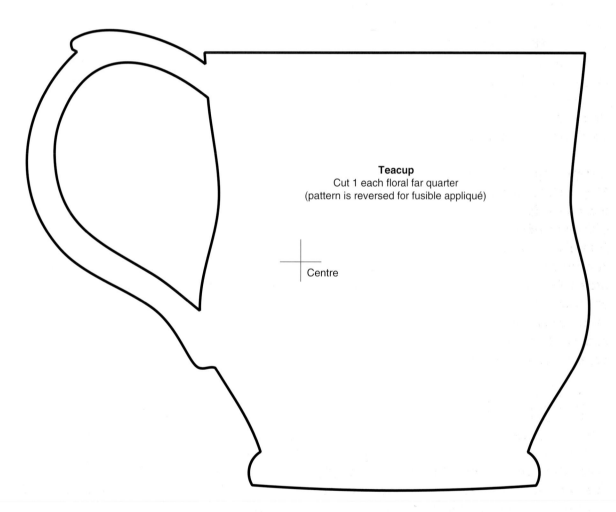

Teacup
Cut 1 each floral far quarter
(pattern is reversed for fusible appliqué)

Centre

Pyramids, or Not?

Look at this quilt once, and it's a group of interlocking six-pointed stars. Look at it again, and it's row after row of pyramids.

BY JANE HERLIHY

Project Specifications
Skill Level: Intermediate
Quilt Size: 42½" x 42½"

Materials
- Light, medium and dark scraps at least 2½" x 7"
- ⅛ yard each purple stripe and purple-with-green dots
- ¼ yard teal-with-purple dots
- ½ yard teal crackle
- Backing 49" x 49"
- Batting 49" x 49"
- Neutral-colour all-purpose thread
- Quilting thread

Instructions
Cutting
Step 1. Prepare templates for A and B using pattern pieces given; cut as directed on each piece, marking dots at seam intersections as marked on patterns.
Step 2. Cut two 1½" x 36½" C strips purple stripe.
Step 3. Cut two 1¾" x 39" D strips purple-with-green dots.
Step 4. Cut two 2½" x 39" E strips teal-with-purple dots.
Step 5. Cut two 2½" x 43" F strips teal crackle.
Step 6. Cut five 2¼" by fabric width strips teal crackle for binding.

Completing the Units
Step 1. Select one each light, medium and dark A piece.
Step 2. Place a light A right sides together with a medium A; match and begin sewing on marked dots from the outside point to the centre referring to Figure 1.

Figure 1   Figure 2

Step 3. Set a dark A piece into the pieced unit to complete one A unit as shown in Figure 2; press seams in the same direction. Repeat for 77 A units, keeping the dark, medium and light A pieces in the same position in every unit.
Step 4. To make corner and side units, join one dark A with one light BR as shown in Figure 3; press seams toward BR. Repeat for four B units.

B Unit Make 4   C Unit Make 3   D Unit Make 4   E Unit Make 3

Figure 3

Step 5. Repeat with a light A and a dark B to complete three C units, a medium A and a light B to complete four D units and a medium A and a

dark BR to complete three E units, again referring to Figure 3.

Completing the Top

Step 1. Arrange one B unit, six A units turned with the dark A on the top, five A units turned with a light A on the bottom and one D unit as shown in Figure 4; join units to make an X row. Repeat for four X rows. Press seams open.

Figure 4

Step 2. Join one C unit, six A units turned with a light A on the bottom, five A units turned with the dark A on top and one E unit as shown in Figure 5; join units to make a Y row. Repeat for three Y rows. Press seams open.

Figure 5

Step 3. Join the rows, beginning with an X row and alternating rows, to complete the pieced top; press seams open.

Step 4. Sew a C strip to the top and bottom, and a D strip to opposite sides of the pieced centre; press seams toward C and D strips.

Step 5. Sew E strips to the top and bottom, and F strips to opposite sides of the pieced centre; press seams toward E and F strips.

Step 6. Layer, quilt and bind referring to the General Instructions. ✦

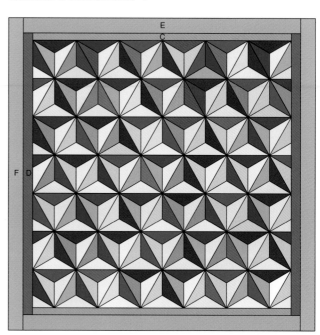

Pyramids, or Not?
Placement Diagram 42¹⁄₂" x 42¹⁄₂"

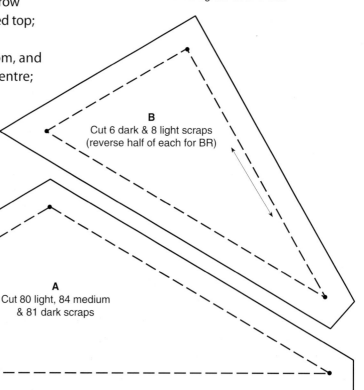

B
Cut 6 dark & 8 light scraps
(reverse half of each for BR)

A
Cut 80 light, 84 medium
& 81 dark scraps

Walk on the Wild Side

Bright-colour mottleds are striking when combined with black.

BY BEA YURKERWICH

Around the World
24" x 24" Block

Project Specifications
Skill Level: Beginner
Quilt Size: 56" x 56"
Block Size: 24" x 24"
Number of Blocks: 4

Materials
- 15 fat quarters bright mottleds
- 1½ yards purple mottled
- 1¾ yards black dot
- Backing 62" x 62"
- Batting 62" x 62"
- Neutral-colour all-purpose thread
- Quilting thread

Instructions
Cutting
Step 1. Prepare templates for A and B pieces using patterns given.

Step 2. Cut one 3⅛" by 22" strip from each fat quarter and purple mottled; subcut four 3⅛" squares from each strip. Use template A to cut curved edge as shown in Figure 1 to make four A pieces from each fabric.

Figure 1

Step 3. Cut two 4½" by 22" strips from each fat quarter and purple mottled; subcut five 4½" squares from each fabric. Use template B to cut away curved area, again referring to Figure 1, to make five B pieces of each fabric.

Step 4. Cut seven 3⅛" by fabric width strips black dot; subcut strips into (80) 3⅛" A squares. Use template A to cut into A pieces.

Step 5. Cut eight 4½" by fabric width strips black dot; subcut strips into (64) 4½" B squares. Use template B to cut into B pieces.

Step 6. Cut six 4½" by fabric width strips purple mottled. Join strips on short ends to make one long strip; subcut strip into two 48½" C strips and two 56½" D strips.

Step 7. Cut six 2¼" by fabric width strips purple mottled for binding.

Completing the Blocks

Figure 2

Step 1. Sew a coloured A to a black B to make an A-B unit as shown in Figure 2; repeat for 64 units.

Step 2. Sew a black A to a coloured B to make a B-A unit, again referring to Figure 2; repeat for 80 units.

Step 3. Arrange and join 16 A-B and 20 B-A units in six rows referring to Figure 3; press seams in adjacent rows in opposite directions. Join these rows to complete one block; press seams in one direction. Repeat for four blocks.

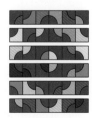

Figure 3

Completing the Top
Step 1. Join two blocks to make a row; press seam to one side. Repeat for two rows.

Step 2. Join the rows to complete the pieced centre; press seam to one side.

Step 3. Sew a C strip to opposite sides, and D strips to the top and bottom of the pieced centre; press seams toward C and D.

Finishing Your Quilt

Step 1. Sandwich the batting between the completed top and prepared backing; pin or baste layers together to hold. ***Note:*** *If using basting spray to hold layers together, refer to instructions on the product container for use.*

Step 2. Quilt as desired by hand or machine; remove pins or basting. Trim excess backing and batting even with quilt top.

Step 3. Join binding strips on short ends to make one long strip. Fold the strip in half along length with wrong sides together; press.

Step 4. Sew binding to quilt edges, mitring corners and overlapping ends. Fold binding to the back side and stitch in place to finish. ✦

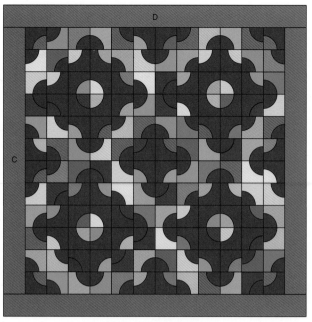

Walk on the Wild Side
Placement Diagram 56" x 56"

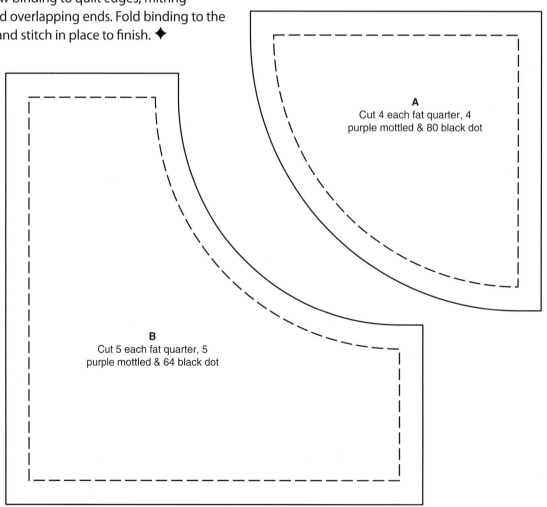

A
Cut 4 each fat quarter, 4
purple mottled & 80 black dot

B
Cut 5 each fat quarter, 5
purple mottled & 64 black dot

Secret Garden

The fabric collection used in this scrappy quilt includes recognizable patterns within a small area—the essence of calico-style prints.

BY MARINDA STEWART FOR SPRINGS

Project Specifications
Skill Level: Beginner
Quilt Size: 40" x 50"

Materials
- Scraps of a variety of light, medium and dark prints at least 4½" long
- Fat eighth navy print
- Scraps light blue, dark blue and brown prints for butterfly
- Scraps yellow plaid, yellow, pink, purple and orange prints for flowers
- ⅛ yard light green print
- ⅛ yard green plaid
- ¼ yard dark brown print
- ¼ yard each blue plaid, blue and cream prints and cream tonal
- ½ yard green print for stems
- ⅝ yard black tonal
- 1 yard black print
- Backing 46" x 56"
- Batting 46" x 56"
- All-purpose thread to match fabrics
- Hand- or machine-quilting thread
- 1 yard fusible web

Instructions
Cutting
Step 1. Prepare templates for appliqué shapes using pattern pieces given.
Step 2. Trace shapes onto the paper side of the fusible web as directed on patterns for total number to cut; cut out shapes, leaving a margin around each one.

Step 3. Fuse shapes to the wrong side of fabrics as directed on patterns for colour; cut out shapes on traced lines. Remove paper backing.

Step 4. Cut 150" total length 1½"-wide bias strips from green print as shown in Figure 1; join strips on short ends with a diagonal seam to make one long stem strip. Fold and stitch strip with wrong sides together along length with a ¼" seam; press strip flat with seam centred and pressed open as shown in Figure 2.

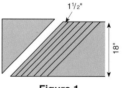

Figure 1   Figure 2

Step 5. Cut pressed stem strip into 11" R, 17" Q, 21" P, 22" O, 24" N and 28" M stem pieces.
Step 6. Cut one 24½" x 34½" A rectangle black print.
Step 7. Cut two 1½" x 24½" B strips and two 1½" x 36½" C strips dark brown print.
Step 8. Cut three strips each 1½" by fabric width blue plaid (D), cream tonal (E), blue print (F) and cream print (G).
Step 9. Cut two 1½" x 30½" H strips and two 1½" x 42½" I strips black tonal.
Step 10. Cut four 4½" x 4½" L squares navy print.
Step 11. Cut a variety of 4½" J/K rectangles from

light, medium and dark print scraps in a variety of widths from 1¼"–1¾." **Note:** *When these strips are joined on the 4½" sides, you will need a total of at least 150" to cut border strips.*

Step 12. Cut five 2¼" by fabric width strips black tonal for binding.

Completing the Quilt

Step 1. Arrange the stem pieces on the A background as desired to create curving stems referring to Figure 3, the Placement Diagram and project photo for positioning ideas.

Figure 3

Step 2. When satisfied with placement; baste to hold in place. Stitch along each folded edge of

Secret Garden
Placement Diagram 40" x 50"

each basted stem piece, turning under exposed ends ⅛"–¼."

Step 3. Arrange leaf shapes along the stitched stems, again referring to the Placement Diagram and project photo. When satisfied with placement, fuse leaves in place.

Step 4. Repeat with petal and centre shapes, and butterfly motif referring to the Placement Diagram and project photo for positioning. **Note:** *Flower centres are different on each flower; arrange as desired.*

Step 5. Repeat with leaves on L squares; place one green plaid and two green print leaves on two squares, and one green print and two green plaid leaves on the remaining two squares.

Step 6. Sew B strips to the top and bottom, and C strips to opposite sides of the appliquéd centre; press seams toward B and C.

Step 7. Sew a D strip to an E strip with right sides together along length; press seams toward D. Repeat for three D-E strip sets.

Step 8. Subcut strip sets into (64) 1½" D-E units as shown in Figure 4.

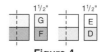

Figure 4

Step 9. Repeat Step 7 with F and G strips to complete three F-G strip sets; subcut strip sets into (68) 1½" F-G units, again referring to Figure 4.

Step 10. Join one D-E unit with one F-G unit to complete a Four-Patch X unit as shown in Figure 5; repeat for 26 units.

X Unit

E	F
D	G

Figure 5

Step 11. Join 13 Four-Patch X units to make a strip as shown in Figure 6; repeat for two strips. Sew a strip to the top and bottom of the pieced centre; press seams toward the B and C strips.

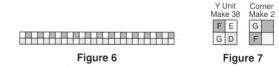

Figure 6

Y Unit
Make 38

F	E
G	D

Corner
Make 2

G	
F	

Figure 7

Step 12. Join one D-E unit with one F-G unit to complete a Four-Patch Y unit as shown in Figure 7; repeat for 38 units.

Step 13. Join two F-G units to complete a corner

Four-Patch unit, again referring to Figure 7; repeat for two units.

Step 14. Join 19 Four-Patch Y units and one corner Four-Patch unit to make a strip as shown in Figure 8; repeat for two strips. Sew these strips to opposite long sides of the pieced centre; press seams toward the B and C strips.

Figure 8

Step 15. Sew H strips to the top and bottom, and I strips to opposite long sides of the pieced centre; press seams toward H and I strips.

Step 16. Select a variety of J/K pieces and join on the 4½" sides to make two 32½" K strips and two 42½" J strips; press seams in one direction.

Step 17. Sew a J strip to opposite long sides of the pieced centre; press seams toward I strips.

Step 18. Referring to the Placement Diagram for positioning, sew an appliquéd L square to each end of each K strip; press seams toward K.

Step 19. Sew a K-L strip to the top and bottom of the pieced centre to complete the top.

Step 20. Satin-stitch around each fused leaf, flower and flower centre, and stitch butterfly antennae using thread to match fabric. ***Note:*** *The appliqué stitching adds quilting at the same time as it secures shapes in place.*

Step 21. Finish the quilt referring to General Instructions. ✦

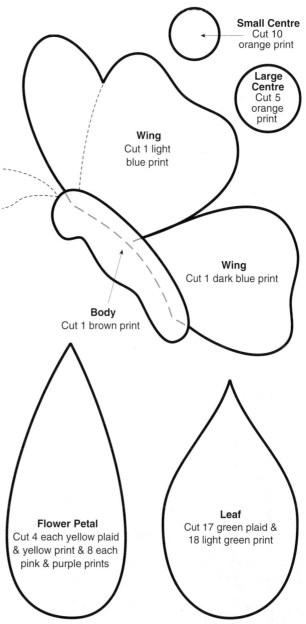

Small Centre
Cut 10
orange print

Large Centre
Cut 5
orange print

Wing
Cut 1 light blue print

Wing
Cut 1 dark blue print

Body
Cut 1 brown print

Flower Petal
Cut 4 each yellow plaid & yellow print & 8 each pink & purple prints

Leaf
Cut 17 green plaid & 18 light green print

Flower Garden Square

Create a grid of squares for the background of the pieced flowers.

BY MARIAN SHENK

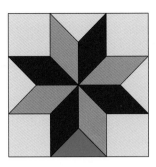

Eight-Pointed Star
7½" x 7½" Block

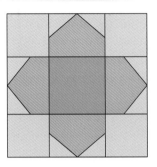

Orange Flower
7½" x 7½" Block

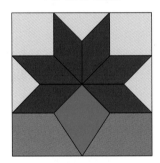

Star Flower
7½" x 7½" Block

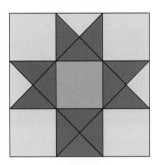

Triangle Flower
7½" x 7½" Block

Project Specifications
Skill Level: Intermediate
Quilt Size: 41" x 36"
Block Size: 7½" x 7½"
Number of Blocks: 4

Materials
- Scraps red, orchid, purple, pink, mauve, salmon and orange fabrics for flowers
- ¼ yard gold print
- ⅜ yard brown tonal
- ½ yard olive green mottled
- ⅝ yard bright green mottled
- ¾ yard blue mottled
- Backing 47" x 42"
- Batting 47" x 42"
- Neutral-colour all-purpose thread
- Quilting thread
- 2 packages brown wide bias tape

Instructions
Making Star Flower Block
Step 1. Prepare templates for all pieces using patterns given; cut as directed on each piece.
Step 2. Cut (10) 2¾" x 2¾" D squares blue mottled.
Step 3. Cut one square bright green mottled and two squares blue mottled 4¼" x 4¼;" cut each square on both diagonals to make A triangles. Discard three bright green and two blue mottled triangles.
Step 4. Sew a red B to a red BR; press seams toward

BR. Set in D between the B points as shown in Figure 1; repeat for two B-D units.

Figure 1   **Figure 2**

Step 5. Join the B-D units as shown in Figure 2; press.
Step 6. Sew an E and ER to C and add a red B and BR as shown in Figure 3; press.

Figure 3   **Figure 4**

Step 7. Join the B-D unit with the B-C-E unit; set in blue A triangles to complete the Star Flower block as shown in Figure 4; press.
Step 8. Set aside remaining pieces for other blocks.

Making Triangle Flower Block
Step 1. Cut one square each bright green and

blue mottleds, and three squares pink scrap 3¾" x 3¾;" cut each square in half on both diagonals to make J triangles. Discard one blue and three bright green triangles.

Step 2. Cut one square mauve scrap and four squares blue mottled 3" x 3" for I.

Step 3. Join one blue and three pink J triangles as shown in Figure 5; repeat for three blue J units. Repeat with one bright green and three pink J triangles to make a green J unit, again referring to Figure 5.

Make 3   Make 1

Figure 5

Step 4. Sew a blue J unit to opposite sides of the mauve I to make a row as shown in Figure 6; press seams toward I.

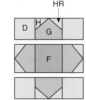

Step 5. Sew a blue I to opposite pink sides of the remaining J units, again referring to Figure 6; press seams toward I.

Figure 6

Step 6. Join the pieced rows to complete the Triangle Flower block, again referring to Figure 6.

Making Orange Flower Block

Step 1. Cut one 3½" x 3½" F square from salmon scrap.

Step 2. Sew H and HR to G; press seams toward H and HR. Repeat for four units.

Step 3. Sew D to opposite sides of two G-H units as shown in Figure 7; press seams toward D. Repeat for two D-G-H rows.

HR

Step 4. Sew a G-H unit to opposite sides of F, again referring to Figure 7; press seams toward F.

Figure 7

Step 5. Join the pieced rows to complete the Orange Flower block, again referring to Figure 7.

Making Eight-Pointed Star Block

Step 1. Join orchid B and purple BR pieces and set in D as for Star Flower block in Figure 1; press. Repeat for four B-D units.

Step 2. Referring to Figure 8, join two B-D units to make a row; repeat. Join B-D rows together as shown in Figure 8; press.

Figure 8

Step 3. Set in 3 blue mottled and 1 bright green A triangles to complete the Eight-Pointed Star block, again referring to Figure 8.

Completing the Top

Step 1. Cut 31 bright green mottled (L), 34 olive green mottled (M) and 67 blue mottled (K) 3" x 3" squares.

Step 2. Arrange the K, L and M squares with the pieced blocks on a flat surface referring to the Placement Diagram. Join to complete the pieced centre; press.

Step 3. Cut two 1½" x 35½" N strips and two 1½" x 32½" O strips gold print. Sew N strips to the top and bottom, and O strips to opposite sides of the pieced centre; press seams toward strips.

Step 4. Cut two 2½" x 37½" P strips and two 2½" x 36½" Q strips brown tonal. Sew P strips to the top and bottom, and Q strips to opposite sides of the pieced centre; press seams toward strips.

Finishing the Quilt

Step 1. Sandwich the batting between the completed top and prepared backing; pin or baste layers together to hold.

Step 2. Hand or machine-quilt as desired. When quilting is complete, trim batting and backing even with top; remove pins or basting.

Step 3. Bind edges with brown wide bias tape to finish. ✦

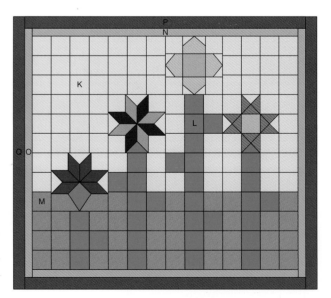

Flower Garden Square
Placement Diagram 41" x 36"

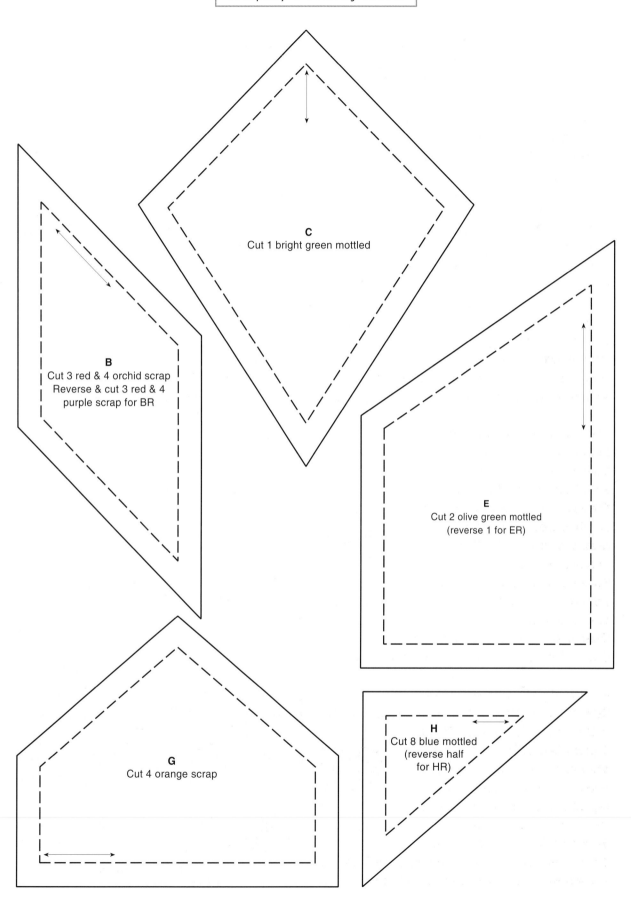

C
Cut 1 bright green mottled

B
Cut 3 red & 4 orchid scrap
Reverse & cut 3 red & 4
purple scrap for BR

E
Cut 2 olive green mottled
(reverse 1 for ER)

G
Cut 4 orange scrap

H
Cut 8 blue mottled
(reverse half
for HR)

Deer Crossing

The sportsman in your life would love this masculine-looking wall quilt.

Deer
11¼" x 11¼" Block

BY JUDITH SANDSTROM

Project Specifications
Skill Level: Beginner
Quilt Size: 48" x 48"
Block Size: 11¼" x 11¼"
Number of Blocks: 4

Materials
- ⅜ yard black mottled
- ½ yard medium blue mottled
- ⅝ yard navy/tan plaid
- 1 yard navy mottled
- 1¼ yards tan-on-tan print
- Batting 54" x 54"
- Backing 54" x 54"
- Neutral-colour and black all-purpose thread
- Tan quilting thread
- ½ yard fusible web
- ⅔ yard fabric stabilizer

Instructions
Making Appliqué Blocks
Step 1. Cut four 11¾" x 11¾" A squares tan-on-tan print; fold and crease to mark diagonal centres.
Step 2. Trace the deer pattern on the paper side of the fusible web four times. *Note: The pattern is already reversed.*
Step 3. Cut out shapes, leaving a margin around each one; fuse shapes to the wrong side of the black mottled. Cut out shapes on traced lines; remove paper backing.
Step 4. Centre a deer shape diagonally on A; fuse in place. Repeat for four blocks.
Step 5. Cut an 11" x 11" square fabric stabilizer; pin a square behind each fused A square.
Step 6. Using black all-purpose thread, machine zigzag-stitch around each deer shape. When stitching is complete, remove fabric stabilizer.

Completing the Top
Step 1. Cut five 2½" by fabric width strips each navy and medium blue mottleds.
Step 2. Sew a navy mottled strip to a medium blue mottled strip with right sides together along length; press seams open. Repeat for five strip sets.
Step 3. Subcut strip sets into 2½" B segments as shown in Figure 1; you will need 80 B segments.
Step 4. Join two B segments as shown in Figure 2 to make B units; press seams open. Repeat for 40 B units. Set aside four B units for borders.
Step 5. Cut three 4⅞" by fabric width strips navy mottled; subcut strips into 4⅞" C squares. You will need 24 squares. Cut each C square in half on one diagonal to make 48 C triangles as shown in Figure 3.

Figure 1   **Figure 2**

Figure 3   **Figure 4**   **Figure 5**

Step 6. Sew a C triangle to a B unit as shown in Figure 4; press seams open. Repeat for 36 B-C units.
Step 7. Stitch a second C triangle to four B-C units as shown in Figure 5; press seams open. Set aside for P units.

Step 8. Join two B-C units as shown in Figure 6 to make M units; repeat for 12 M units. Press seams open.

M unit
Make 12

Figure 6

Step 9. Sew C to four M units to make N units as shown in Figure 7; press seams open.

N unit
Make 4

Figure 7

O unit
Make 4

Figure 8

P unit
Make 4

Figure 9

Step 10. Sew C to four M units to make O units as shown in Figure 8.

Step 11. Join two B-C units with a C-B-C unit set aside in step 7 to make a P unit as shown in Figure 9; press seams open; repeat for four P units.

Step 12. Cut two 9¼" x 9¼" D squares tan-on-tan print. Cut each D square in half on both diagonals to make D triangles as shown in Figure 10.

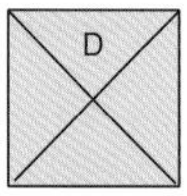

D

Figure 10

Step 13. Sew a D triangle to opposite sides of each remaining M unit as shown in Figure 11.

Step 14. Lay out the pieced units with the appliquéd blocks referring to Figure 12; join units using set-in seams where necessary; press seams open.

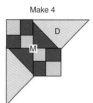

Make 4

Figure 11

Figure 12

Step 15. Cut four 4½" x 40½" E strips navy/tan plaid.

Step 16. Sew an E strip to opposite sides of the pieced centre; press seams toward strips. Sew the remaining B units to each end of each remaining E strip; press seams open.

Step 17. Sew the B-E strips to the remaining sides of the pieced centre; press seams open.

Finishing the Quilt

Step 1. Sandwich batting between the completed top and prepared backing piece; pin or baste layers together to hold flat for quilting.

Step 2. Quilt as desired by hand or machine. **_Note: The quilt shown was hand-quilted ¼" from seams using tan quilting thread._**

Step 3. When quilting is complete, trim batting and backing even with quilted top; remove pins or basting.

Step 4. Cut five 2¼" by fabric width strips tan-on-tan print; join strips on short ends to make one long strip for binding.

Step 5. Fold the binding strip in half along length with wrong sides together; press.

Step 6. Sew binding strip to quilt edge with raw edges matching, mitring corners and overlapping beginning and end; turn to backside. Hand or machine-stitch in place to finish. ✦

Deer Crossing
Placement Diagram 48" x 48"

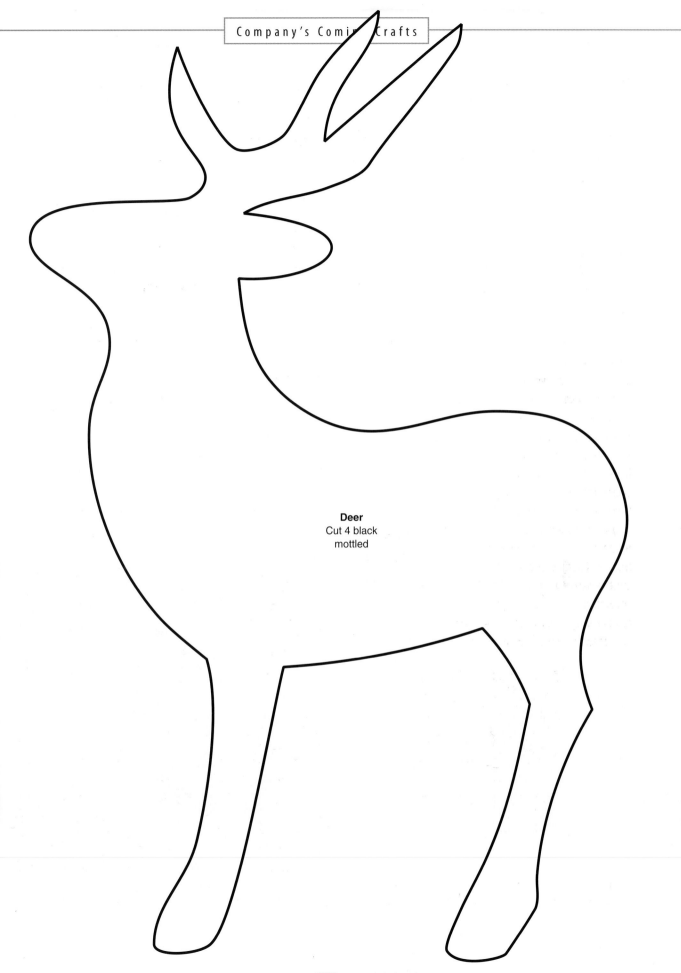

Deer
Cut 4 black
mottled

Autumn Ridge Lap Quilt

Scraps in the colours of autumn leaves make a pretty seasonal lap quilt.

BY PEARL LOUISE KRUSH

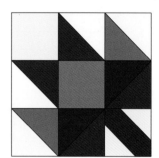

Green Maple Leaf
9" x 9" Block

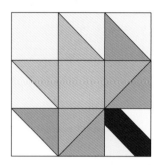

Rust/Brown Maple Leaf
9" x 9" Block

Tan/Gold Maple Leaf
9" x 9" Block

Project Specifications
Skill Level: Beginner
Quilt Size: 53" x 71"
Block Size: 9" x 9"
Number of Blocks: 35

Materials
- Scraps of 5 tan/gold fabrics to total 1 yard
- Scraps of 5 green fabrics to total ¾ yard
- Scraps of 5 rust/brown fabrics to total ⅞ yard
- ½ yard brown print for stems
- ½ yard green mottled for borders
- ½ yard brown/rust print for binding
- ¾ yard autumn print for borders
- Scraps white/cream fabrics to total 1¾ yards
- Backing 59" x 77"
- Batting 59" x 77"
- Neutral-colour all-purpose thread
- Quilting thread

Instructions
Cutting
Step 1. Cut 10 green, 12 brown/rust and 13 tan/gold 3½" x 3½" A squares and 35 white/cream 3½" x 3½" B squares.

Step 2. Cut 70 white/cream 3⅞" x 3⅞" C squares; cut each square in half on one diagonal to make C triangles.

Step 3. Cut 40 green, 48 rust and 52 gold 3⅞" x 3⅞" D squares; cut each square in half on one diagonal to make D triangles.

Step 4. Cut 35 brown print F squares 3½" x 3½."

Step 5. Cut 70 white/cream E squares 2½" x 2½;" draw a line from corner to corner on the wrong side of each square.

Step 6. Cut six strips 1½" by fabric width green mottled; join strips on short ends to make one long strip. Press seams open. Cut strip into two 63½" G strips and two 47½" H strips.

Step 7. Cut six strips 3½" by fabric width autumn print; join strips on short ends to make one long strip. Press seams to one side. Cut strip into two 65½" I strips and two 47½" J strips.

Step 8. Cut four 3½" x 3½" K squares green mottled.

Step 9. Cut seven 2¼" by fabric width strips brown/rust print for binding.

Piecing the Blocks
Step 1. Separate the cut pieces into piles by colour families and shapes.

Step 2. To piece one green block, select four same-fabric pairs of D triangles.

Step 3. Sew C to D and D to D as shown in Figure 1; repeat for four C-D and two D-D units.

Figure 1

Step 4. Place an E square on F and stitch on the marked line as shown in Figure 2; trim seam to ¼" and press E to the right side. Repeat on the opposite corner of F with a second E to complete an E-F unit as shown in Figure 3.

Figure 2   **Figure 3**

Step 5. Arrange the C-D and D-D units with A and B squares and the E-F unit in rows as shown in Figure 4; join units to make rows. Press seams in adjacent rows in opposite directions.

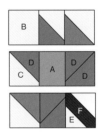

Figure 4

Step 6. Join the rows to complete one green Maple Leaf block, again referring to Figure 4; press seams in one direction.

Step 7. Repeat with tan/gold, rust/brown and remaining green pieces to complete 10 green, 12 rust/brown and 13 tan/gold blocks.

Completing the Top

Step 1. Arrange blocks in seven rows of five blocks each referring to the Placement Diagram for positioning of blocks. ***Note:*** *In the sample quilt, the blocks are arranged with same-colour blocks creating diagonal rows across the quilt top.*

Step 2. Join blocks in rows; press seams in adjacent rows in opposite directions. Join the rows to complete the pieced centre; press seams in one direction.

Step 3. Sew a G strip to opposite long sides, and H strips to the top and bottom of the pieced centre; press seams toward strips.

Step 4. Sew an I strip to opposite long sides of the pieced centre; press seams toward I.

Step 5. Sew a K square to each end of each J strip; press seams toward J. Sew a J-K strip to the top and bottom of the pieced centre; press seams toward J-K strips.

Finishing the Quilt

Step 1. Sandwich the batting between the completed top and prepared backing; pin or baste layers together to hold.

Step 2. Hand or machine-quilt as desired. When quilting is complete, trim batting and backing even with top; remove pins or basting.

Step 3. Join the previously cut binding strips on short ends to make one long strip. Fold the strip in half along length with wrong sides together; press.

Step 4. Sew binding to quilt edges, mitring corners and overlapping ends. Fold binding to the back side and stitch in place to finish. ✦

Autumn Ridge Lap Quilt
Placement Diagram 53" x 71"

Stardust in the Cabin

Use planned fabrics for this scrappy-looking quilt or take the opportunity to use up some real scraps in the design.

BY RHONDA TAYLOR

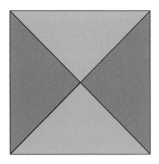

Large X
8½" x 8½" Block

Log Cabin
8½" x 8½" Block

Project Specifications
Skill Level: Intermediate
Quilt Size: 43" x 60"
Block Size: 8½" x 8½"
Number of Blocks: 15

Materials
- ¼ yard each 6 light prints
- ¼ yard each 6 dark prints
- ¾ yard blue floral
- 1 yard red print
- 1 yard each blue and gold tonals
- Backing 49" x 66"
- Batting 49" x 66"
- All-purpose thread to match fabrics
- Hand- or machine-quilting thread

Project Note
The designer used foundation patterns to make half and quarter Log Cabin units for the outer edges and corners. These patterns included small triangles at the ends of some strips as can be seen in the straight-on photo of the quilt. We have eliminated these small triangles and used plain strips on side and corner triangle patterns to simplify piecing.

Instructions
Cutting
Step 1. Assign a letter A–F to each of the six light prints and a letter G–L to each of the six dark prints.

Step 2. Cut one 3½" by fabric width strip red print for piece 1 of Log Cabin units.

Step 3. Cut two 5½" x 5½" squares red print; cut each square on both diagonals to make triangles for piece 1 of Side Triangles.

Step 4. Cut four 2½" x 4½" rectangles red print for piece 2 of Corner Triangles.

Step 5. Cut two 2" by fabric width strips each light prints A and B and dark prints G and H.

Step 6. Cut three 2" by fabric width strips each light prints C and D and dark prints I and J; subcut each strip into 8" segments for piece 1 of Corner Triangles.

Step 7. Cut two 2½" by fabric width strips each light prints E and F and dark prints K and L; cut each strip into 4½" segments for piece 2 of Corner Triangles.

Step 8. Cut five squares each gold tonal (M) and blue tonal (N) 9¾" x 9¾;" cut each square in half on both diagonals to make M and N triangles. Discard two gold triangles.

Step 9. Cut four squares blue tonal (O) and six squares gold tonal (P) 5⅛" x 5⅛;" cut each square on one diagonal to make O and P triangles.

Step 10. Cut (and piece) two 1" x 51½" Q and two 1" x 35½" R strips red print.

Step 11. Cut and piece two 4½" x 52½" S and two 4½" x 43½" T strips blue floral.

Step 12. Cut six 2¼" by fabric width strips red print for binding.

Piecing Corner Triangles

Step 1. Make 52 copies of the Corner Triangle Foundation Pattern. Be sure the lines are visible on both sides of the paper.

Step 2. Centre a light print D strip right side up over piece 1 on the unmarked side of one pattern; pin a light print F strip right sides together with D as shown in Figure 1.

| Figure 1 | Figure 2 |

Step 3. Turn the pattern over and stitch on the marked line between pieces 1 and 2 as shown in Figure 2; trim seam allowance to ¼" and press the F piece over to cover piece 2, again referring to Figure 2.

Step 4. Trim the excess fabric and paper even with the outside solid line of the pattern to complete one Corner Triangle. Repeat to make 52 Corner Triangles referring to Figure 3 for fabric combinations. *Note: Use the previously cut red print rectangles and cut one 8" segment each from the A, B, G and H strips to complete the four red print Corner Triangles.*

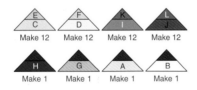

Figure 3

Piecing Log Cabin Blocks

Step 1. Sew the red print 3½"-wide strip to a light print A strip with right sides together along length; press seam toward red print. Subcut strip set into eight 3½" segments as shown in Figure 4.

Figure 4

Step 2. Sew the pieced units to a light print B strip as shown in Figure 5; cut apart even with the

original pieced unit as shown in Figure 6. Press seams toward the B strip.

| Figure 5 | Figure 6 |

Step 3. Add dark print G and H strips to the pieced unit in the same way to complete eight Log Cabin units as shown in Figure 7; press seams toward the last added strip.

Figure 7   Figure 8

Step 4. Sew a Corner Triangle to each edge of the Log Cabin unit to complete 1 block as shown in Figure 8; press seams toward the Corner Triangles. Repeat to make eight Log Cabin Blocks.

Piecing Large X Blocks

Figure 9

Step 1. Sew M to N as shown in Figure 9; press seams toward N. Repeat for 14 M-N units.

Step 2. Join two M-N units to complete one Large X block, again referring to Figure 9; press seam in one direction. Repeat for seven blocks.

Piecing Border Units

Step 1. Make six copies of the Side Triangle Foundation Pattern as directed on the full-size pattern.

Step 2. Cut the following 6"-long segments for piece 2 from the remaining A, B and G strips: three A, two B and one G.

Step 3. Cut the following 7"-long segments for piece 3 from the remaining B, G and H strips: one B, two G and three H.

Step 4. Using these strips and the previously cut red print triangles for piece 1, complete four Side Triangles and two reversed Side Triangles as shown in Figure 10. Trim excess fabric and paper even with the solid outer line on the pattern.

Make 1

Make 1

Make 2

Reversed
Make 2

Figure 10

Step 5. Sew a Corner Triangle to each angled edge of the Side Triangles to complete six edge units as shown in Figure 11; press seams toward the Corner Triangles.

Make 1

Make 1

Make 2

Make 2

Figure 11

Step 6. Join two Corner Triangles to make a corner unit as shown in Figure 12; press seam in one direction. Repeat to make four corner units, again referring to Figure 12.

Figure 12

Step 7. Sew O to each short side of M to make an M-O unit as shown in Figure 13; repeat for four M-O units. Repeat with N and P triangles to make six N-P units, again referring to Figure 13.

Make 4

Make 6

Figure 13

Completing the Top

Step 1. Join two Log Cabin blocks, one Large X block and two N-P units to make a row as shown in Figure 14; press seams away from Log Cabin blocks. Repeat for three rows.

Make 3

Make 2
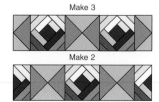

Figure 14

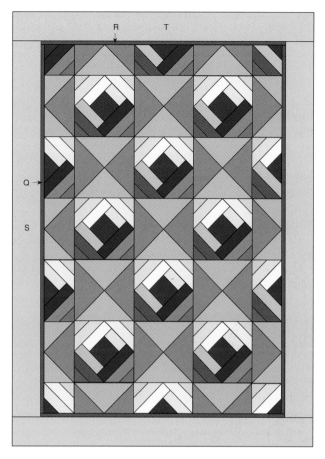

Stardust in the Cabin
Placement Diagram 43" x 60"

Step 2. Join one Log Cabin block, two Large X blocks and two edge units to make a row, again referring to Figure 14; press seams toward Large X blocks. Repeat for two rows.

Step 3. Join two M-O units, one edge unit and two corner units to make an end row as shown in Figure 15; press seams toward M-O. Repeat for two end rows.

Figure 15

Step 4. Arrange rows and join referring to the Placement Diagram for positioning to complete the pieced centre; press seams in one direction.

Step 5. Sew a Q strip to opposite long sides and an R strip to the top and bottom of the pieced centre; press seams toward strips.

Step 6. Sew an S strip to opposite long sides and a T strip to the top and bottom of the pieced centre to complete the top; press seams toward strips.

Step 7. Remove all paper foundations.

Finishing the Quilt

Step 1. Sandwich the batting between the completed top and prepared backing; pin or baste layers together to hold.

Step 2. Hand or machine-quilt as desired. When quilting is complete, trim batting and backing even with top; remove pins or basting.

Step 3. Join binding strips on short ends to make one long strip. Fold the strip in half along length with wrong sides together; press.

Step 4. Sew binding to quilt edges, mitring corners and overlapping ends. Fold binding to the backside and stitch in place to finish. ✦

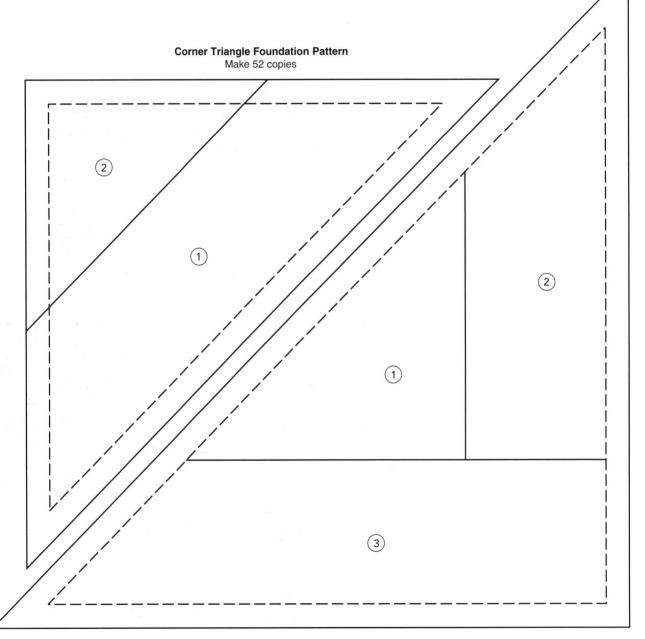

Corner Triangle Foundation Pattern
Make 52 copies

Side Triangle Foundation Pattern
Make 6 copies
(reverse 2)

Four Seasons

Choose scraps with lots of contrast to create the blocks in this scrappy quilt.

BY CARLA SCHWAB

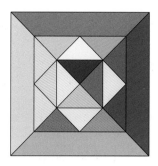

Four Seasons
12" x 12" Block

Project Specifications
Skill Level: Beginner
Quilt Size: 36" x 48"
Block Size: 12" x 12"
Number of Blocks: 12

Materials
- Scraps of 3 or more blue, gold and tan prints
- Scraps of 4 or more light and dark green prints
- Scraps of 4 different yellow solids from medium to dark
- ½ yard dark print for binding
- Backing 42" x 54"
- Batting 42" x 54"
- Neutral-colour all-purpose thread
- Quilting thread

Instructions
Step 1. Prepare templates for A and B using patterns given. Cut as directed on each piece for one block; repeat for 12 blocks.

Step 2. Join three A triangles from one colour group with one yellow A referring to the Placement Diagram and photo of quilt for colour suggestions, and to Figure 1 for piecing. Repeat for four A units, one from each colour group; press.

Figure 1

Figure 2

Step 3. Sew B to each A unit as shown in Figure 2; press seams toward B. **Note:** *Sew light green B*

pieces to the darker yellow A units and dark green B pieces to the lighter yellow A units.

Step 4. Join two light green A-B units as shown in Figure 3; press seams open. Repeat with two dark green A-B units; join to complete one block as shown in Figure 4; press seams open.

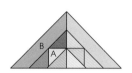

Figure 3

Figure 4

Step 5. Repeat Steps 1–4 to complete 12 blocks.

Step 6. Arrange blocks in four rows of three blocks each; press seams in one direction.

Step 7. Join the rows to complete the pieced top.

Finishing the Quilt

Step 1. Sandwich the batting between the completed top and prepared backing; pin or baste layers together to hold.

Step 2. Hand or machine-quilt as desired. When quilting is complete, trim batting and backing even with top; remove pins or basting.

Step 3. Cut five 2¼" by fabric width strips dark print for binding. Join strips on short ends to make one long strip. Fold the strip in half along length with wrong sides together; press.

Step 4. Sew binding to quilt edges, mitring corners and overlapping ends. Fold binding to the backside and stitch in place. ✦

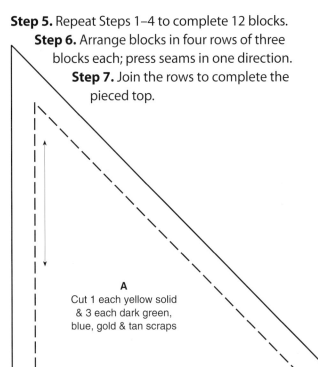

A
Cut 1 each yellow solid
& 3 each dark green,
blue, gold & tan scraps

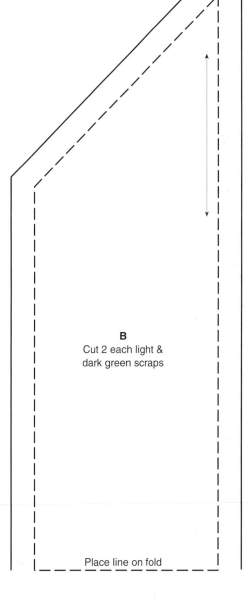

B
Cut 2 each light &
dark green scraps

Place line on fold

Four Seasons
Placement Diagram 36" x 48"

Tossed Triangles

Collect a bunch of different plaid fabrics and create triangle/square units to join randomly in this simple wall quilt.

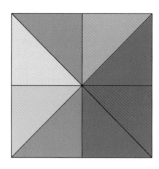

Tossed Triangles
12" x 12" Block

BY LYNDA MILLIGAN AND NANCY SMITH OF POSSIBILITIES

Project Specifications
Skill Level: Beginner
Quilt Size: 56" x 56"
Block Size: 12" x 12"
Number of Blocks: 16

Materials
- ¼ yard each of 14 different plaid fabrics
- ¾ yard multi-plaid
- ¾ yard multi-stripe
- Backing 62" x 62"
- Batting 62" x 62"
- Neutral-colour all-purpose thread
- Hand- or machine-quilting thread

Instructions
Piecing the Top
Step 1. Cut four or five 6⅞" x 6⅞" squares of each plaid fabric for a total of 64 squares.
Step 2. Cut each square in half on one diagonal to make 128 A triangles.
Step 3. Select two different A triangles and join on the diagonal to make an A-A unit referring to Figure 1; repeat for all A triangles to create 64 A-A units.

Figure 1   **Figure 2**   **Figure 3**

Step 4. Select four A-A units; join two units as shown in Figure 2; repeat. Join two A units to complete one block as shown in Figure 3. Repeat for 16 blocks.

Completing the Top
Step 1. Join four blocks to complete one row as shown in Figure 4; repeat for four rows. Press seams in one direction.

Figure 4

Step 2. Join the rows, alternating pressed seam allowance direction. Press seams in one direction between rows.
Step 3. Cut five 1½" by fabric width strips multi-stripe; join strips on short ends to make one long strip. Press seams in one direction.
Step 4. Cut strip into two 48½" B strips and two 50½" C strips. Sew B to opposite sides and C to the top and bottom of the pieced centre; press seams toward strips.
Step 5. Cut six 3½" by fabric width strips multi-plaid; join strips on short ends to make one long strip. Press seams in one direction.
Step 6. Cut strip into two 50½" D strips and two 56½" E strips. Sew D to opposite sides and E to the

top and bottom of the pieced centre; press seams toward strips.

Finishing the Quilt

Step 1. Sandwich the batting between the completed top and prepared backing.

Step 2. Hand- or machine-quilt as desired. When quilting is complete, trim batting and backing even with top. ***Note:*** *The quilt shown was machine-quilted as shown in Figure 5.*

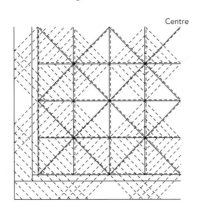

Figure 5

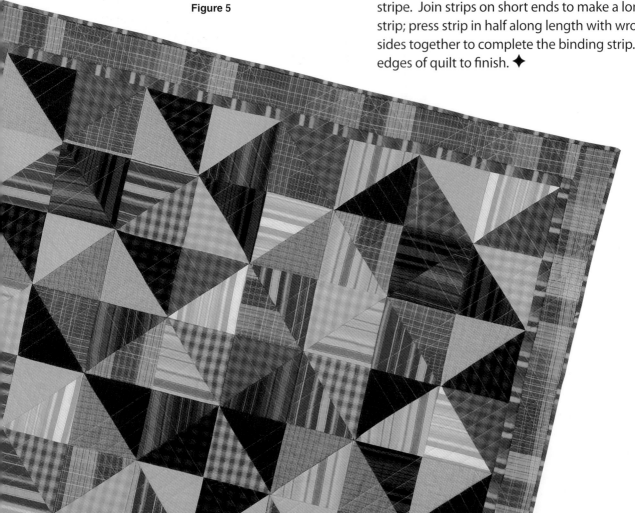

Tossed Trianlges
Placement Diagram 56" x 56"

Step 3. Cut six 2¼" by fabric width strips multi-stripe. Join strips on short ends to make a long strip; press strip in half along length with wrong sides together to complete the binding strip. Bind edges of quilt to finish. ✦

Mexicali Rose

Imagine a trip south of the border as you relax with this lap-size quilt.

BY MICHELE CRAWFORD

Mexicali Rose A
14" x 14" Block

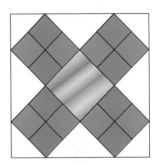

Mexicali Rose B
14" x 14" Block

Project Specifications
Skill Level: Beginner
Quilt Size: 55" x 69"
Block Size: 14" x 14"
Number of Blocks: 12

Materials
- ½ yard each blue, green, pink/red and yellow tonals
- ⅜ yard Southwestern print
- 1½ yards white tonal
- 2⅛ yards yellow floral
- Backing 61" x 75"
- Batting 61" x 75"
- White, rose pink, yellow and green all-purpose thread
- Yellow and pink machine-quilting and craft thread
- Basting spray

Instructions
Cutting
Step 1. Cut two 6" x 44½"K strips, two 6" x 69½" L strips and four 2¼" x 69" binding strips along the length of the yellow floral.

Step 2. Cut six 5½" x 5½" on-point squares Southwestern print for A. Cut six 5½" x 5½" B squares from remaining width of yellow floral.

Step 3. Cut four strips each pink/red (C), yellow (D), green (G) and blue (H) tonals 3" by fabric width.

Step 4. Cut three 8⅜" by fabric width strips white tonal; subcut strips into (12) 8⅜" E squares. Cut each square in half on both diagonals to make (48) E triangles.

Step 5. Cut three 4⅜" by fabric width strips white tonal; subcut strips into (24) 4⅜" F squares. Cut each square in half on one diagonal to make (48) F triangles.

Step 6. Cut six 1½" by fabric width strips white tonal; join strips on short ends to make one long strip. Subcut strip into two 42½" I strips and two 58½" J strips.

Piecing the Blocks

Step 1. Sew a C strip to a D strip and a G strip to an H strip with right sides together along length; press seams toward darker strips. Repeat for four strip sets each combination.

Step 2. Subcut strip sets into 3" segments as shown in Figure 1 to make 48 each C-D and G-H units.

Figure 1   **Figure 2**

Step 3. Join two C-D units as shown in Figure 2; repeat for 24 units. Repeat to complete 24 G-H units, again referring to Figure 2. Press seams in one direction.

Step 4. Sew E and F triangles to one C-D unit as shown in Figure 3; press seams toward E and F. Repeat for 12 units. Repeat with E and F and G-H units, again referring to Figure 3.

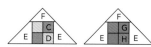

Figure 3

Step 5. Sew a C-D unit to opposite sides of A and add F as shown in Figure 4; press seams toward A and F. Repeat with G-H, B and F, again referring to Figure 4.

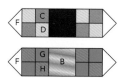

Figure 4

Step 6. To complete blocks, join the pieced units as shown in Figure 5; repeat to complete six each blocks A and B. Press seams toward centre units.

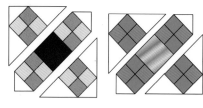

Figure 5

Completing the Top

Step 1. Join two A blocks with one B block to make a row; press seams toward A blocks. Repeat for two rows.

Step 2. Join two B blocks with one A block to make a row; press seams toward A block. Repeat for two rows.

Step 3. Join the rows referring to the Placement Diagram; press seams in one direction.

Step 4. Sew an I strip to the top and bottom, and J strips to opposite sides of the pieced centre; press seams toward I and J.

Step 5. Sew a K strip to the top and bottom, and L strips to opposite sides of the pieced centre; press seams toward K and L.

Step 6. Finish quilt referring to the General Instructions, using basting spray to hold layers together, and machine-quilting and craft thread for quilting. ◆

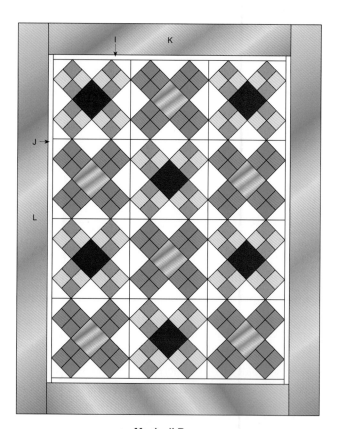

Mexicali Rose
Placement Diagram 55" x 69"

Prairie Points Throw

Star points are formed by the 3-D prairie points stitched around the edges of the yellow squares.

BY CHRIS MALONE

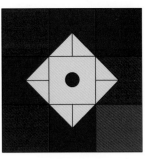

Prairie Points Star
9" x 9" Block

Project Notes

The sample uses 10 assorted yellow prints or tonals for making the star units, making three complete stars from each fabric. The red background squares are cut from a wide assortment of fabrics for a scrappy look. Thirty squares may be cut from a fat quarter.

Project Specifications

Skill Level: Beginner
Quilt Size: 45" x 54"
Block Size: 9" x 9"
Number of Blocks: 30

Materials

- ½ yard red mottled for binding
- 1½ yards total yellow tonals or prints
- 2¼ yards total red tonals, prints or mottleds
- Backing 51" x 60"
- Batting 51" x 60"
- All-purpose thread to match fabrics
- Quilting thread
- 30 assorted red ⅞" buttons
- Spray starch

Instructions
Cutting

Step 1. Cut five matching 3½" x 3½" yellow A squares; repeat to cut 30 sets (150 squares total).

Step 2. Cut (240) 3½" x 3½" red B squares.
Step 3. Cut five 2¼" by fabric width strips red mottled for binding.

Completing the Star Units

Step 1. Fold an A square in half with wrong sides together; press. Find the centre of the folded edge and make two diagonal folds down from this point, creating a triangle with a vertical fold in the centre to complete a prairie point as shown in Figure 1; press. Spray with spray starch; press again. Repeat for four matching prairie points.

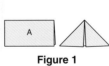

Figure 1   **Figure 2**

Step 2. Pin one folded prairie point with vertical fold against the right side of a matching A square and raw edges even; baste ⅛" from raw edge to hold in place. Repeat with the remaining prairie points as shown in Figure 2 to complete a star unit.
Step 3. Repeat Steps 1 and 2 to complete 30 star units.

Completing the Prairie Points Star Blocks

Step 1. To complete one block, sew a B square to the right and left side of a star unit as shown in

Figure 3; press seams open to reduce bulk. Press side prairie points toward B.

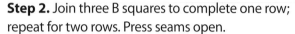

Figure 3   Figure 4

Step 2. Join three B squares to complete one row; repeat for two rows. Press seams open.

Step 3. Join the rows to complete one block as shown in Figure 4; press seams open and prairie points toward B. Repeat for 30 blocks.

Completing the Top

Step 1. Join five blocks to make a row; repeat for six rows. Press seams in one direction.

Step 2. Join the rows to complete the quilt top.

Step 3. Complete the quilt referring to General Instructions.

Prairie Points Star Throw
Placement Diagram
45" x 54"

Completing Your Quilt

Step 1. Sandwich the batting between the completed top and prepared backing; pin or baste layers together to hold. **Note:** *If using basting spray to hold layers together, refer to instructions on the product container for use.*

Step 2. Quilt as desired by hand or machine; remove pins or basting. Trim excess backing and batting even with quilt top.

Step 3. Join binding strips on short ends to make one long strip. Fold the strip in half along length with wrong sides together; press.

Step 4. Sew binding to quilt edges, mitring corners and overlapping ends. Fold binding to the back side and stitch in place to finish.

Step 5. Sew a red button to the centre of each A square of each block to complete the quilt. ✦

Irish Dresden Plate

The Dresden Plate is the perfect pattern for using up lots of scraps. In this quilt, both the blocks and the border shapes will go far toward emptying your scrap basket.

BY BARBARA CLAYTON

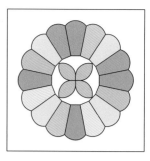

Dresden Plate
12" x 12" Block

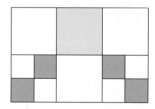

Irish Chain
12" x 12" Block

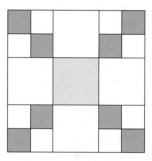

Half Irish Chain
12" x 8" Block

Project Note

The quilt shown has a planned scrappy look that uses light and medium shades of blue, green and pink. Because the fabrics are cut in strips to eliminate one step of the cutting/stitching process, the plate pieces in the sample were not cut from hundreds of scraps. If you have a large variety of scraps, this quilt would look lovely with a less planned look.

Project Specifications

Skill Level: Intermediate
Quilt Size: Approximately 66½" x 91"
Block Size: 12" x 12" and 12" x 8"
Number of Blocks: 15 and 10

Materials

- ⅛ yard each pink solid and medium blue tonal for petals
- ¼ yard total light blue scraps
- ½ yard total light green and medium blue scraps
- ⅞ yard blue-and-white gingham
- 1 yard medium green tonal
- 1¾ yards total pink scraps
- 5 yards white solid
- Backing 73" x 97"
- Batting 73" x 97"
- Neutral-colour all-purpose thread
- Quilting thread
- Clear nylon monofilament
- 1½ yards fusible interfacing
- Stylet

Instructions

Making Dresden Plate Blocks

Step 1. Cut eight white solid A squares 12½" x 12½" for blocks. Fold and crease squares horizontally, vertically and diagonally to mark block centres.

Step 2. Cut 2½" by fabric width strips as follows: one light blue scrap, four each light green scraps, medium green tonal, blue-and-white gingham and medium blue scraps, and 17 pink scraps.

Step 3. Sew a pink strip to a medium green strip with right sides together along length; press seam toward darker strip. Repeat to make four strip sets. Repeat to make one light blue/pink and four sets each light green/pink, gingham/pink and medium blue/pink. Press seams toward darker fabrics.

Step 4. Prepare a template for the B Unit using pattern given.

Step 5. Place the B Unit template on the sewn strips, lining up the straight line between B pieces with the seam between the strips as shown in Figure 1. Cut the following B units: eight light blue/pink, 32 gingham/pink, 36 each medium green/pink and light green/pink, and 40 medium blue/pink. Set aside 20 each medium green/pink and light green/pink, and 24 each gingham/pink and medium blue/pink for borders.

Figure 1

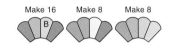

Make 16   Make 8   Make 8

Figure 2

Step 6. Sew a medium green/pink B unit to a light green/pink B unit to make a quarter unit as shown in Figure 2. Repeat to make 16 green/pink quarter units, again referring to Figure 2. Sew a medium blue/pink B unit to a light blue/pink B unit; repeat for eight quarter units. Repeat with medium blue/pink and gingham/pink B units to make eight quarter units, again referring to Figure 2.

Step 7. Join two quarter units as shown in Figure 3; repeat. Join these halves to complete one Dresden Plate unit, again referring to Figure 3. Press joining seams in one direction. Repeat for four green/pink and four blue/pink Dresden Plate units.

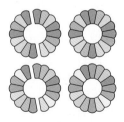

Figure 3

Step 8. Pin the Dresden Plate units to the lightweight fusible interfacing with the right side of the fabric toward the fusible side of the interfacing. Cut out the interfacing around outside edge of plate units.

Step 9. Stitch around the outside curved edges of the plate units and the inside circle edge using a ¼" seam allowance.

Step 10. Trim away the interfacing in centre circle

and around outer edge to match the plate unit; clip curves and inverted points.

Step 11. Cut through the centre of the interfacing above the B pieces all the way around the plate unit as shown in Figure 4; turn right side out through the opening.

Figure 4

Figure 5

Step 12. Using a broken pencil or stylet, smooth the curved edges.

Step 13. Centre and pin one plate unit to an A square, using crease lines as guides for placement as shown in Figure 5; press shapes in place to fuse.

Step 14. Using clear nylon monofilament and a machine blind-hem stitch, sew around the outside and inside edge of each plate unit.

Step 15. Prepare petal template using pattern given; cut as directed on the piece.

Step 16. Pin the petals to the lightweight fusible interfacing and cut out as for plate units; stitch around outside edges using a ¼" seam allowance. Cut a slit in the interfacing side of each stitched petal; turn right side out. Smooth as for plate units.

Step 17. Centre four blue petals in the blue blocks and four pink petals in the green blocks referring to the block drawing for positioning; fuse and stitch in place as for plate units.

Completing the Irish Chain Blocks

Step 1. Cut seven strips white solid 4½" by fabric width; subcut into (58) 4½" C squares.

Step 2. Cut two strips blue-and-white gingham 4½" by fabric width; subcut into (17) 4½" x 4½" D squares.

Step 3. Cut six strips each white solid (E) and medium green tonal (F) 2½" by fabric width. Sew a white strip to a green strip with right sides together along length; press seams toward darker fabric. Subcut strip sets into (96) 2½" E-F units.

Step 4. To complete one Irish Chain block, join two E-F units as shown in Figure 6; press seams in one direction. Repeat for four units.

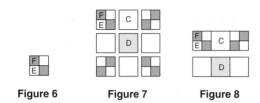

| Figure 6 | Figure 7 | Figure 8 |

Step 5. Arrange the E-F units with C and D squares in rows referring to Figure 7. Join in rows; press seams away from C squares. Join the rows to complete one Irish Chain block; press seams toward D row. Repeat for seven blocks.

Step 6. To make Half Irish Chain blocks, join two E-F units with one D and three C squares as shown in Figure 8; press as for whole blocks. Repeat for 10 half blocks.

Completing the Pieced Centre

Step 1. Cut four 8½" x 8½" G squares and six 8½" x 12½" H rectangles white solid.

Step 2. Join two G, one H and two half blocks to make a row as shown in Figure 9; repeat for two rows. Press seams toward G and H.

Figure 9

Step 3. Join two half blocks with one Irish Chain block, and one each blue and green Dresden Plate blocks to make a row as shown in Figure 10; press seams toward Dresden Plate blocks. Repeat to make 3 rows.

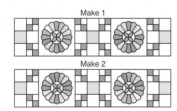

Figure 10

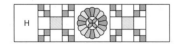

Figure 11

Step 4. Join two H rectangles with two Irish Chain blocks and one green Dresden Plate block to make

a row as shown in Figure 11; repeat for another row with a blue block. Press seams toward Dresden Plate blocks.

Step 5. Arrange pieced rows as shown in Figure 12; join rows to complete the pieced centre.

Figure 12

Completing the Pieced Border

Step 1. Cut and piece two 8½" x 52½" I strips and two 8½" x 92½" J strips white solid. Sew the I strips to the top and bottom and the J strips to opposite long sides of the pieced centre; press seams toward strips.

Step 2. Prepare templates for B and K using patterns given; cut as directed on each piece.

Step 3. Using B units set aside in Making Dresden Plate Blocks, sew a medium green/pink B unit to a light green/pink B unit; add a medium green B to the pink end to complete one green shell unit as shown in Figure 13; press. Repeat to make 20 shell units.

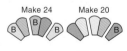

Figure 13

Step 4. Join two medium blue/pink B units and add a gingham B to the pink end to complete one blue shell unit, again referring to Figure 13; press. Repeat to make 24 shell units.

Step 5. Join the shell units, alternating blue and green shells as shown in Figure 14. *Note: The blue shells curve outward and the green shells curve inward.* You will need two strips with seven blue and six green shells for the side borders, and two strips with five blue and four green shells for the top and bottom borders.

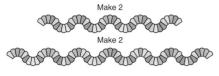

Figure 14

Figure 15

Step 6. Sew a medium green KR to a pink K to make a corner unit as shown in Figure 15; press. Repeat for four corner units.

Step 7. Join the top and bottom, and side border strips with the corner units to make a rectangle as shown in Figure 16.

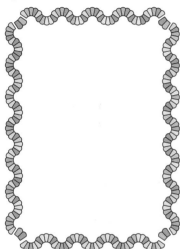

Figure 16

Step 8. Stitch a turning guideline ¼" from the inside and outside edges all around pieced rectangle.

Step 9. Place the rectangle on the I/J border strips with the innermost green pieces approximately ¾" from the I/J border seam line as shown in Figure 17. ***Note:*** *Adjust seams between pieces as necessary to make fit.*

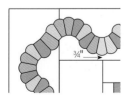

¾"

Figure 17

Step 10. Fold under the inside raw edges along the stitched guideline and pin in place on border strips, clipping curves as you pin.

Step 11. Stitch the inside edge of the rectangle to the border strips with clear nylon monofilament using a blind-hem stitch as for the Dresden Plate blocks. Trim away the excess white border fabric from behind and beyond the pieced border after stitching is complete as shown in Figure 18.

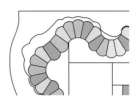

Figure 18

Finishing the Quilt

Step 1. Lay the batting on a flat surface; lay the prepared backing on the batting right side up. Lay the quilt top right sides together with backing. Smooth layers and baste or pin to hold flat.

Irish Dresden Plate
Placement Diagram
Approximately 66½" x 91"

Step 2. Sew around the outside curved edges, leaving about a 10" opening for turning.

Step 3. Trim excess batting and backing even with top edges; clip each curve and inverted point. Turn right side out through opening. Smooth edges with stylet.

Step 4. Turn under the edges at the opening ¼" and slipstitch opening closed. Lightly press the border edges.

Step 5. Hand- or machine-quilt ¼" from edge of quilt.

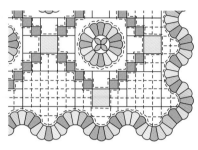

Figure 19

Step 6. Hand- or machine-quilt as desired referring to Figure 19 for suggestions. ✦

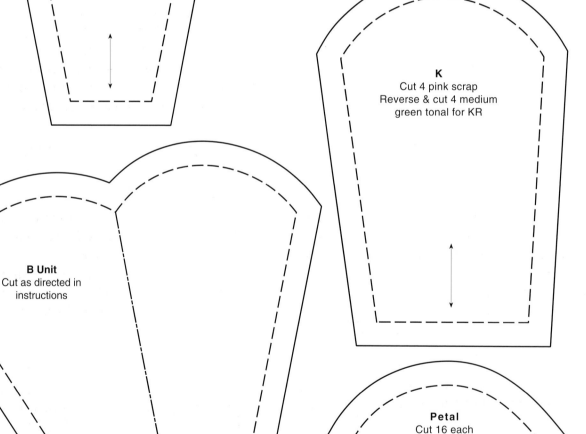

B
Cut 20 medium green tonal & 24 blue-and-white gingham

K
Cut 4 pink scrap
Reverse & cut 4 medium green tonal for KR

B Unit
Cut as directed in instructions

Petal
Cut 16 each medium blue tonal & pink solid

Triangle Plaids

A variety of woven and printed plaids are used to create movement in this bed-size quilt.

BY CONNIE KAUFFMAN

Project Specifications
Skill Level: Intermediate
Quilt Size: 78" x 104"

Materials
- 80 (7⅜" x 7⅜") light plaid squares for A
- 80 (7⅜" x 7⅜") dark plaid squares for B
- ⅔ yard dark plaid for binding
- 1 yard total red and rust scraps for borders
- 1 yard total dark green scraps for borders
- Backing 84" x 110"
- Batting 84" x 110"
- Neutral-colour all-purpose thread
- Quilting thread

Instructions
Step 1. Cut each A and B square in half on one diagonal to make 160 A and 160 B triangles.
Step 2. Sew A to B to complete an A-B unit as shown in Figure 1; repeat for 148 A-B units. Press seams toward B.

| Figure 1 | Figure 2 |

Step 3. Sew A to A to complete an A-A unit, again referring to Figure 1; repeat for four A-A units. Press seams to one side.
Step 4. Cut four 4" x 23" C strips dark green scraps and four 3½" x 23" D strips red or rust scraps.
Step 5. Sew a C strip to a D strip with right sides together along length; press seams to one side. Repeat for four C-D strips.

Step 6. Align a B triangle on one end of a C-D strip as shown in Figure 2; stitch along the diagonal of B and press B to the right side. Trim away excess C-D from behind B as shown in Figure 3. Repeat for two B-C-D and two B-C-D reversed strips.

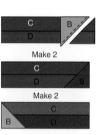

Make 2

Make 2

Figure 3

Step 7. Join one B-C-D and one B-C-D reversed strip as shown in Figure 4 to make a top border strip; press seams open. Repeat for a bottom border strip.

Figure 4

Step 8. Cut six 4" x 26½" E strips dark green scraps and two 3½" x 26½" F strips red or rust scraps. Cut four 3½" x 20" G strips red or rust scraps.
Step 9. Sew an E strip to a G strip with right sides together along length, leaving 8" from the end of E unstitched as shown in Figure 5. Repeat for four E-G strips.

| Figure 5 | Figure 6 |

Step 10. Sew a B triangle to one end of each strip referring to Step 6 and Figure 6 to make two B-E-G and two B-E-G reversed strips.

Step 11. Sew an E strip to an F strip with right sides together along length; press seam to one side. Repeat for two E-F strips.

Step 12. Sew a B triangle to each end of the E-F strips as shown in Figure 7 to make two B-B-E-F strips.

Figure 7

Step 13. Join one B-E-G strip and one B-E-G reversed strip with a B-B-E-F strip as shown Figure 8 to make a side border strip; press seams open. Repeat for two strips.

Figure 8

Step 14. Lay out the A-A and A-B units, A triangles and border strips as shown in Figure 9. *Note: The A-A units are in the inner corners and the A triangles form the outer corners.* Join centre A-B and A-A units to make rows; join rows to complete the pieced centre.

Figure 9

Step 15. Sew the B-C-D strips to the top and bottom of the pieced centre; press seams toward B-C-D.

Step 16. Sew a side border strip to opposite sides of the pieced centre; finish unstitched seam between E and G strips at ends and complete side seam as shown in Figure 10. Press seams toward side border strips.

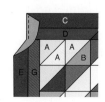

Figure 10

Step 17. Join side A-B units to make rows; join rows and sew to opposite sides of the pieced centre; press seams toward side border strips.

Step 18. Join top and bottom A triangles and A-B units to make rows; join rows and sew to the top and bottom of the pieced centre; press seams toward B-C-D strips to complete the pieced top.

Finishing the Quilt

Step 1. Sandwich the batting between the completed top and prepared backing piece; pin or baste to hold.

Step 2. Hand- or machine-quilt as desired.

Step 3. Trim batting and backing even with the quilted top.

Step 4. Cut nine 2¼" by fabric width strips dark plaid for binding.

Step 5. Join the binding strips on short ends with a diagonal seam to make a long strip; press seams toward one side.

Step 6. Press the strip in half along length with wrong sides together to complete the binding strip. Bind edges of quilt to finish. ✦

Triangle Plaids
Placement Diagram 78" x 104"

Mill Wheel Stripes

Make a quick bed-size quilt using a variety of brightly-coloured stripes.

Mill Wheel
8" x 8" Block

BY RUTH SWASEY

Project Specifications
Skill Level: Intermediate
Quilt Size: 85½" x 97"
Block Size: 8" x 8"
Number of Blocks: 42

Materials
- ½ yard each of 13 different stripe fabrics
- 3⅔ yards cream mottled
- 3⅞ yards blue mottled
- Backing 92" x 103"
- Batting 92" x 103"
- Neutral-colour all-purpose thread
- Hand- or machine-quilting thread

Instructions
Cutting
Step 1. Cut two strips each 3½" x 91½" (D) and 3½" x 86" (E) along the length of the blue mottled.
Step 2. Cut 10 strips blue mottled 8½" by remaining fabric width and five strips 8½" by fabric width; subcut strips into 8½" squares for A. You will need 56 A squares.
Step 3. Cut 39 strips cream mottled 3¼" by fabric width for B.
Step 4. Cut three 3⅜" by fabric width strips from each of the 13 stripe fabrics for C.
Step 5. Cut nine 2¼" by fabric width strips from remaining stripe fabrics for binding.

Completing the Blocks
Step 1. Sew a B strip to a C strip with right sides

together along length; press seam toward C strip. Repeat with all B and C strips.
Step 2. Using the B-C template given, cut each strip into B-C triangle units referring to Figure 1; repeat for all B-C strip sets.

Figure 1

Step 3. Select two same-fabric B-C units. Join the two units as shown in Figure 2 to complete a half-block unit; press seams in one direction. Repeat for 26 half-block units.

Figure 2

Step 4. Select four same-fabric B-C units; join two units as shown in Figure 2; repeat. Press seams in one direction.
Step 5. Join the two B-C sections as shown in Figure 3 to complete one block; repeat for 42 blocks. Press seams in one direction.

Figure 3

Step 6. Select four B-C units from the remaining units for quarter blocks.

Completing the Top

Step 1. Arrange and join the A squares and whole, half and quarter blocks in diagonal rows referring to Figure 4; press seams toward A squares.

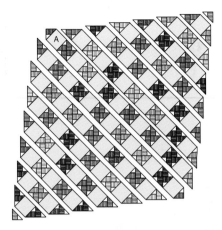

Figure 4

Step 2. Join the pieced rows to complete the quilt centre.

Step 3. Sew a D strip to opposite sides, and an E strip to the top and bottom of the pieced centre; press seams toward strips.

Finishing the Quilt

Step 1. Sandwich the batting between the completed top and prepared backing.

Step 2. Hand or machine-quilt as desired. When quilting is complete, trim batting and backing even with top.

Step 3. Join the previously cut 2¼"-wide stripe strips on short ends to make one long strip; press seams open. Fold the strip along length with wrong sides together; press. Sew strips to the quilt top, mitring corners and overlapping ends to finish. ✦

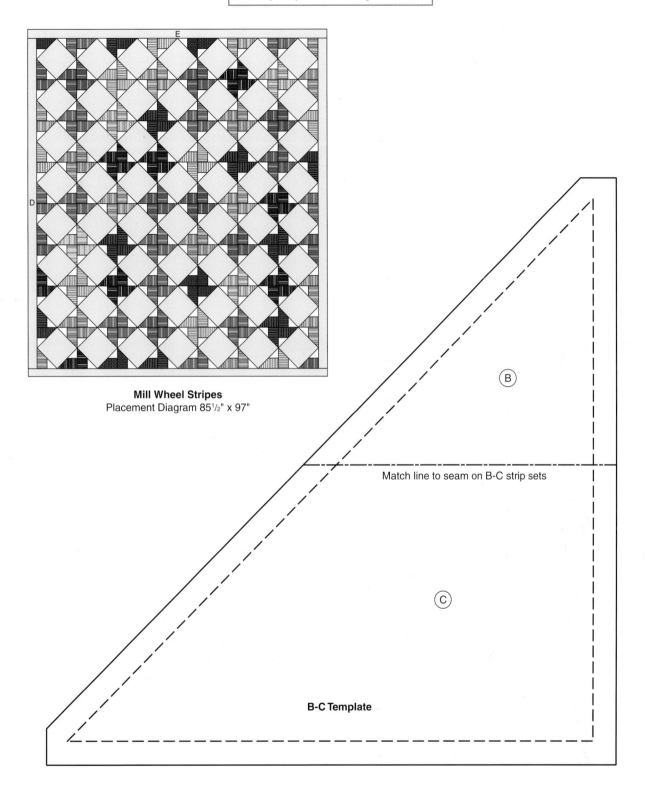

Mill Wheel Stripes
Placement Diagram 85½" x 97"

Ⓑ

Match line to seam on B-C strip sets

Ⓒ

B-C Template

Graceful Baskets

Whether you choose to make every basket different, the same or in a combination of colours, this bed-size quilt is simple to piece.

BY JUDITH SANDSTROM

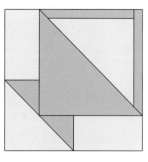

Graceful Basket
12" x 12" Block

Project Specifications
Skill Level: Beginner
Quilt Size: 96½" x 113½"
Block Size: 12" x 12"
Number of Blocks: 50

Materials
- ¾ yard each 10 tonals, stripes or florals
- 1¾ yards rose tonal
- 2 yards blue tonal
- 6¼ yards cream tonal
- Backing 102" x 119"
- Batting 102" x 119"
- All-purpose thread to match fabrics

Instructions
Cutting
Step 1. Prewash and iron all fabrics before cutting.
Step 2. Cut seven 9⅞" by fabric width strips cream tonal; subcut strips into (25) 9⅞" squares. Cut each square in half on one diagonal to make 50 A triangles.
Step 3. Cut nine 6½" by fabric width strips cream tonal; subcut into (100) 3½" B rectangles.
Step 4. Cut five 6⅞" by fabric width strips cream tonal; subcut strips into (25) 6⅞" squares. Cut each square in half on one diagonal to make 50 C triangles.
Step 5. Cut one 9⅞" by fabric width strip from each of the 10 fabrics, and blue and rose tonals; cut two 9⅞" D squares from each of the 10 fabric strips and

three 9⅞" D squares each from blue and rose tonal strips. Cut all squares in half on one diagonal to make D triangles. Set aside one each blue and rose tonal triangles for another project.
Step 6. Cut four 3⅞" x 3⅞" E squares and four each 1¼" x 11" F and G strips from each of the 10 fabrics and five E 3⅞" x 3⅞" squares and five each F and G 1¼" x 11" strips each blue and rose tonals. Cut each E square in half on one diagonal to make 100 E triangles.
Step 7. Cut three 18¼" by fabric width strips cream tonal; subcut strips into five 18¼" H squares. Cut each square in half on both diagonals to make 20 H triangles. Set aside two triangles for another project.
Step 8. Cut two 9⅜" x 9⅜" I squares cream tonal; cut each square in half on one diagonal to make I triangles.
Step 9. Cut eleven 2" by fabric width strips rose tonal; join strips on short ends to make one long strip. Cut two 102½" J strips, two 97" K strips and four 4¾" O rectangles from the strip.
Step 10. Cut two 5⅛" x 5⅛" squares blue tonal; cut each square in half on one diagonal to make four L triangles.
Step 11. From nine of the 10 fabrics cut one 9¾" by fabric width strip; cut one 9¾" M square from six strips and two 9¾" M squares from three strips. Cut each M square in half on both diagonals to make 48 M triangles. Set aside four triangles for another project.

Step 12. Cut three 9¾" by fabric width strips blue tonal; subcut strips into (10) 9¾" N squares. Cut each square in half on both diagonals to make 40 N triangles.

Step 13. Cut four 4¾" x 4¾" P squares blue tonal.

Step 14. Cut eleven 2¼" by fabric width strips rose tonal for binding.

Making Basket Blocks

Step 1. To piece one block, select same-fabric D, E, F and G pieces.

Step 2. Mark a line ¾" from edge on each short side of A as shown in Figure 1. Pin F to A with raw edge along marked line and matching one end as shown in Figure 2.

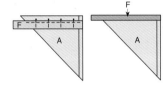

Figure 1   Figure 2

Graceful Baskets
Placement Diagram 96½" x 113½"

Step 3. Stitch in place ¼" from raw edge of F. Press F to the right side, again referring to Figure 2.

Step 4. Repeat with G and trim ends even with A as shown in Figure 3.

Figure 3

Figure 4

Step 5. Sew E to B; repeat for two B-E units as shown in Figure 4; press seams toward B.

Step 6. Referring to Figure 5, sew B-E units to D; press seams toward B-E units. Add C.

Figure 5

Figure 6

Step 7. Sew a B-C-D-E unit to the A-F-G unit to complete one block referring to Figure 6; repeat for 50 blocks.

Completing the Top

Step 1. Arrange and join the blocks in diagonal rows with H and I triangles referring to the Placement Diagram. Press seams in adjacent rows in opposite directions.

Step 2. Join 12 M and 11 N triangles; add L to each end to make a side strip as shown in Figure 7. Press seams toward L and N. Repeat for two side strips.

Figure 7

Step 3. Sew a side strip to J; press seam toward J. Repeat for two strips. Sew a strip to opposite long sides of the pieced centre; press seams toward J.

Step 4. Sew K to the top and bottom of the pieced centre; press seams toward K.

Step 5. Join 10 M and nine N triangles; add L to each end to make a top strip. Repeat for bottom strip. Press seams toward L and N. Sew O and P to each end of each strip as shown in Figure 8; press seams toward O and P.

Figure 8

Step 6. Sew strips to the top and bottom of the pieced centre; press seams toward K to complete the pieced top.

Finishing the Quilt

Step 1. Sandwich the batting between the completed top and prepared backing; pin or baste layers together to hold.

Step 2. Hand or machine-quilt as desired. When quilting is complete, trim batting and backing even with top; remove pins or basting.

Step 3. Join binding strips on short ends to make one long strip. Fold the strip in half along length with wrong sides together; press.

Step 4. Sew binding to quilt edges, mitring corners and overlapping ends. Fold binding to the back side and stitch in place. ✦

Jewel Basket

The scrappy jewel-like appearance of the basket tops is actually created with planned placement of fabrics in this late-1800s antique quilt and the matching pillow.

FROM SUE HARVEY

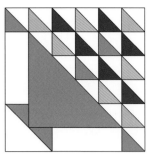

Jewel Basket
10½" x 10½" Block

Antique Quilt

Project Specifications
Skill Level: Intermediate
Quilt Size: 74" x 89"
Block Size: 10½" x 10½"
Number of Blocks: 20

Materials
- ¼ yard blue plaid
- ⅓ yard each red dot and gold solid
- 1 yard green print
- 2⅔ yards pink print
- 5¼ yards off-white solid
- Backing 80" x 95"
- Batting 80" x 95"
- White all-purpose thread
- Quilting thread

Instructions
Cutting
Step 1. Cut two strips each 4" x 91" (O) and 4" x 76" (P) along length of pink print.
Step 2. Cut three 2⅝" by remaining fabric width strips pink print; subcut into (26) A squares.
Step 3. Cut 1"-wide pink print bias strips to equal 350."
Step 4. Cut three 2⅝" by fabric width strips green print; subcut into (44) 2⅝" B squares.
Step 5. Cut two 7⅝" by fabric width strips green

print; subcut into (10) 7⅞" squares. Cut each square on one diagonal to make 20 H triangles.
Step 6. Cut two 2⅝" by fabric width strips green print; subcut into (20) 2⅝" squares. Cut each square on one diagonal to make 40 J triangles.
Step 7. Cut two 2⅝" by fabric width strips blue plaid; subcut into (20) 2⅝" C squares.
Step 8. Cut three 2⅝" by fabric width strips gold solid; subcut into (40) 2⅝" D squares.
Step 9. Cut three 2⅝" by fabric width strips red dot; subcut into (40) 2⅝" E squares.
Step 10. Cut two strips each 4" x 91" (Q) and 4" x 76" (R) along length of off-white solid.
Step 11. Cut (19) 2⅝" by remaining fabric width strips off-white solid; subcut into (170) 2⅝" F squares.
Step 12. Cut four 3¾" by remaining fabric width strips off-white solid; subcut into (20) 3¾" squares. Cut each square on both diagonals to make 80 G triangles.
Step 13. Cut four 5¾" by remaining fabric width strips off-white solid; subcut into (40) 2¼" I rectangles.
Step 14. Cut two 4⅜" by fabric width strips off-white solid; subcut into (10) 4⅜" squares. Cut each square on one diagonal to make 20 K triangles.
Step 15. Cut four 11" by fabric width strips off-white solid; subcut into (12) 11" L squares.
Step 16. Cut four 16⅛" squares off-white solid;

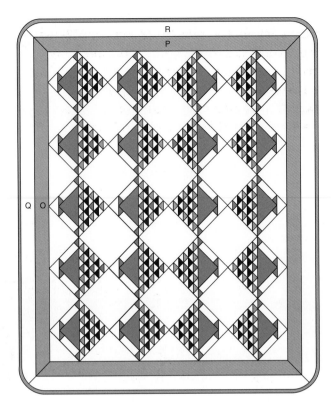

Jewel Basket Quilt
Placement Diagram 74" x 89"

cut each square on both diagonals to make 16 M triangles. Set aside two triangles for another use.
Step 17. Cut two 8⅜" squares off-white solid; cut each square on one diagonal to make four N triangles.

Piecing Blocks

Step 1. Draw a diagonal line from corner to corner on the wrong side of each F square.
Step 2. Place an A square right sides together with an F square, stitch ¼" on each side of the marked line, cut apart on the line and press A to the right side to make two A-F units as shown in Figure 1.

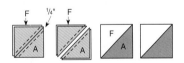

Figure 1

Step 3. Repeat Step 2 with all A, B, C, D and E squares to make 52 A-F, 88 B-F, 40 C-F, 80 D-F and 80 E-F units.
Step 4. To piece one block, join two each B-F, D-F and E-F units in rows with four G triangles as shown

in Figure 2; press seams away from the F triangles. Join the rows to complete the top basket unit.

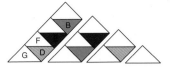

Figure 2

Step 5. Sew J to one end of I as shown in Figure 3; press seam toward J. Repeat for two I-J units.

Figure 3

Step 6. Sew I-J to adjacent sides of H as shown in Figure 4; press seams toward H.
Step 7. Sew K to the J edge of the pieced unit, again referring to Figure 4; press seam toward K to finish the bottom basket unit.

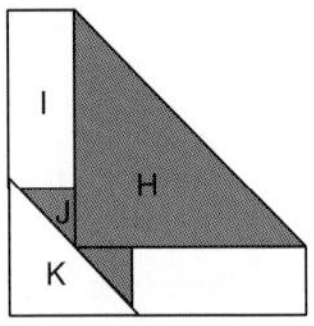

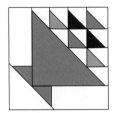

Figure 4

Step 8. Join the top and bottom basket units as shown in Figure 5; press seam toward H.

Figure 5

Figure 6

Step 9. Join one each colour F unit to make a row as shown in Figure 6; press seams away from F triangles. Repeat with one each B-F, C-F, D-F and E-F units and two A-F units to make a row, again referring to Figure 6.

Step 10. Sew the pieced rows to adjacent sides of the basket unit to complete one Jewel Basket block as shown in Figure 7; repeat to make 12 blocks with a pink top-corner unit and eight blocks with a green top-corner unit as shown in Figure 8.

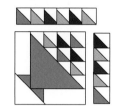

Figure 7

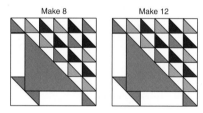

Figure 8

Completing the Top

Step 1. Join the blocks in diagonal rows with the L squares and M and N triangles as shown in Figure 9; press seams away from the pieced blocks. One A-F unit will not be used for block.

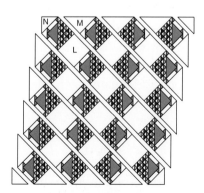

Figure 9

Step 2. Join the rows to complete the pieced centre; press seams in one direction.

Step 3. Sew an O strip to a Q strip; press seam toward O. Repeat for two strips. Repeat with P and R strips.

Step 4. Sew the O-Q strips to opposite long sides and the P-R strips to the top and bottom of the pieced centre, mitring corners. Press corner seams open and border seams toward strips to complete the top.

Step 5. Use a plate to trim each corner into a gently rounded shape as shown in Figure 10.

Figure 10

Finishing the Quilt

Step 1. Sandwich the batting between the completed top and prepared backing; pin or baste to hold.

Step 2. Quilt as desired by hand or machine, stopping 1" away from the outside edge.

Step 3. Trim backing even with the quilted top and batting ¼" smaller; remove pins or basting.

Step 4. Turn top and backing edges in ¼;" press lightly to hold.

Step 5. Join the 1"-wide pink print bias strips with diagonal seams to make a long strip; press seams open.

Step 6. Fold strip in half along length with wrong sides together.

Step 7. Beginning on one long edge, insert strip between top and backing layers with batting between layers of strip and folded edge of strip extending ¼" beyond top and backing edges as shown in Figure 11; pin in place. Cut off end of strip, leaving ½" extending over beginning end as shown in Figure 12. Turn under strip end ¼," covering beginning end. Hand-stitch along folded edge.

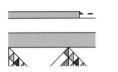

Figure 11

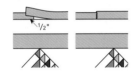

Figure 12

Step 8. Topstitch close to folded edge of the quilt top through all layers as shown in Figure 13; repeat for a second line of stitching a scant ¼" from the first line to complete the quilt.

Figure 13

Pillow

Project Specifications

Skill Level: Intermediate
Pillow Size: 26" x 26" (including flange)
Block Size: 10½" x 10½"
Number of Blocks: 1

Materials

• ⅛ yard each red dot, blue plaid and gold solid
• ⅓ yard green print
• ¾ yard pink solid
• 1¾ yards off-white solid
• Batting 28" x 28"
• White all-purpose thread
• White quilting thread
• Basting spray
• 18" pillow form

Instructions

Cutting

Step 1. Cut 2⅝" squares as follows: one blue plaid (C), two each pink solid (A), green print (B), gold solid (D) and red dot (E) and nine off-white solid (F).

Step 2. Cut one 7⅞" square green print; cut on one diagonal to make two H triangles. Set aside one triangle for another use.

Step 3. Cut one 2⅝" square green print; cut on one diagonal to make two J triangles.

Step 4. Cut one 3¾" square off-white solid; cut on both diagonals to make four G triangles.

Step 5. Cut two 2¼" x 5¾" I rectangles off-white solid.

Step 6. Cut one 4⅜" square off-white solid; cut on one diagonal to make two K triangles. Set aside one triangle for another use.

Step 7. Cut two 8⅜" squares off-white solid; cut on one diagonal to make four L triangles.

Step 8. Cut four 4" x 28" N strips off-white solid.

Step 9. Cut two 15½" x 26½" pieces off-white solid for backing.

Step 10. Cut four 2¼" x 28" M strips pink solid.

Step 11. Cut 1"-wide pink solid bias strips to equal 130."

Completing the Top

Step 1. Complete one Jewel Basket block with a pink top-corner unit referring to Piecing Blocks for Antique Quilt. One A-F unit will not be used for block.

Step 2. Sew an L triangle to each side of the pieced block as shown in Figure 14; press seams toward triangles.

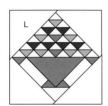

Figure 14

Step 3. Sew an M strip to an N strip; press seam toward M. Repeat for four M-N strips. Sew a strip to each side of the block unit, mitring corners. Press corner seams open and border seams toward strips.

Step 4. Use a plate to trim each corner in a gently rounded shape as for quilt in Figure 10.

Finishing the Pillow

Step 1. Apply basting spray to one side of the batting square; place the pieced top wrong side against the sprayed batting and smooth.

Step 2. Hand or machine-quilt as desired, stopping 1" away from the outer edge.

Step 3. Trim the batting ¼" smaller all around than the quilted top.

Step 4. Turn under one 26½"-long edge of each backing piece ¼;" turn under again ½" and topstitch to hem.

Step 5. Place the backing pieces wrong sides against the batting side of the quilted top, overlapping the backing pieces 3" as shown in Figure 15; pin in place.

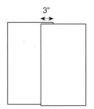

Figure 15

Step 6. Turn in the edges of the quilted top and the backing pieces ¼;" press lightly to hold.

Step 7. Apply folded bias strip to edges as for Antique Quilt in Steps 5–8 of Finishing the Quilt.

Step 8. Stitch in the ditch of the pink and off-white border seams through all layers to make the flange.

Step 9. Insert pillow form through back opening to complete the pillow. ◆

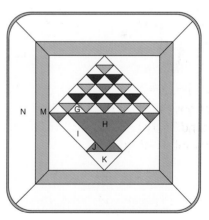

Jewel Basket Pillow
Placement Diagram 26" x 26"
(including flange)

Sunlit Scraps

Careful placement of light, medium and dark values creates the design in this bed-size flannel quilt.

BY SUE HARVEY

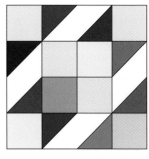

Sunny Lanes Variation A
20" x 20" Block

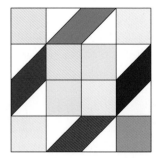

Sunny Lanes Variation B
20" x 20" Block

Project Specifications
Skill Level: Beginner
Quilt Size: 95" x 95"
Block Size: 20" x 20"
Number of Blocks: 16

Materials
- ⅞ yard cream tonal flannel for border
- ⅞ yard total dark flannel binding fabrics
- 3½ yards total light flannel scraps
- 4 yards total medium flannel scraps
- 5½ yards total dark flannel scraps
- Backing 101" x 101"
- Batting 101" x 101"
- Neutral-colour all-purpose thread
- Quilting thread

Instructions
Cutting
Step 1. Cut 128 squares 5½" x 5½" medium scraps for A.

Step 2. Cut 32 rectangles 5½" x 10½" light scraps for B.

Step 3. Cut 64 squares 5½" x 5½" light scraps for E.

Step 4. Cut 64 squares 5½" x 5½" dark scraps for C.

Step 5. Cut 32 rectangles 5½" x 10½" dark scraps for D.

Step 6. Cut eight strips 3" by fabric width cream tonal; set aside for F and G borders.

Step 7. Cut 10 strips 2½" by fabric width from binding fabrics.

Step 8. Cut remaining dark scraps in 5½"-wide, random-length strips; set aside for H and I borders.

Piecing Blocks
Step 1. Draw a diagonal line from corner to corner on the wrong side of each C and E square.

Step 2. Place a C square right sides together on one end of a B rectangle; stitch on the marked line, trim seam allowance to ¼" and press C to the right side as shown in Figure 1.

Figure 1

Step 3. Repeat on the remaining end of B to complete one B-C unit, again referring to Figure 1. Repeat to make 16 B-C units.

Step 4. Repeat Steps 2 and 3 to make 16 reversed B-C units as shown in Figure 2.

Figure 2

Step 5. Repeat Steps 2 and 3 using D and E pieces to complete 16 each D-E and reversed D-E units, again referring to Figure 2.

Step 6. Join two A squares to make a row; press seam to one side. Repeat for 32 A rows.

Step 7. Join two A rows to complete a centre unit as shown in Figure 3; press seam to one side. Repeat for 16 centre units.

Figure 3

Step 8. To piece one Sunny Lanes Variation A block, sew a reversed B-C unit to opposite sides of a centre unit to make a row as shown in Figure 4; press seams toward B-C.

Figure 4

Figure 5

Step 9. Sew an A square to each end of a B-C unit to make a row as shown in Figure 5; press seams toward B-C. Repeat for two rows.

Step 10. Join the rows to complete one A block as shown in Figure 6; press seams toward the outer rows. Repeat for 8 A blocks.

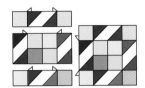

Figure 6

Step 11. Repeat Steps 7–9 to complete one Sunny Lanes Variation B block using D-E and reversed D-E units as shown in Figure 7, except press seams toward the A centre unit, the A squares and the centre rows; repeat for 8 B blocks.

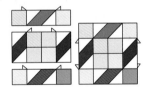

Figure 7

Completing the Top

Step 1. Join two A blocks with two B blocks to make a row as shown in Figure 8; repeat for four rows. Press seams in one direction in each row.

Step 2. Join the rows to complete the pieced centre referring to the Placement Diagram for positioning of rows. Press seams open between rows.

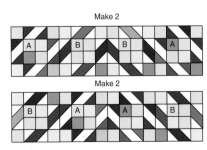

Make 2

Make 2

Figure 8

Step 3. Join the F/G border strips on short ends to make a long strip; cut into two 80½"-long F strips and two 85½"-long G strips.

Step 4. Sew the F strips to opposite sides, and the G strips to the remaining sides; press seams toward strips.

Step 5. Join the H/I strips on short ends to make a strip 370" long; cut into two 85½"-long H strips and two 95½"-long I strips.

Step 6. Sew the H strips to opposite sides, and the I strips to the remaining sides; press seams toward strips to complete the top.

Finishing the Quilt

Step 1. Sandwich the batting between the completed top and prepared backing piece; pin or baste to hold.

Step 2. Hand or machine-quilt as desired.

Step 3. Trim batting and backing even with the quilted top.

Step 4. Join the binding strips on short ends with a diagonal seam to make a long strip; press seams toward one side.

Step 5. Press the strip in half along length with wrong sides together to complete the binding strip. Bind edges of quilt to finish. ✦

Sunlit Scraps
Placement Diagram 95" x 95"

Random Colours

Bright novelty prints are tied together with black solids in this colourful quilt.

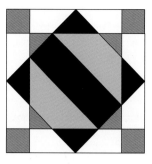

Random Colours
12" x 12" Block

BY CONNIE RAND

Project Specifications
Skill Level: Beginner
Quilt Size: 64" x 76"
Block Size: 12" x 12"
Number of Blocks: 20

Materials
- ½ yard binding fabric
- ¾ yard total bright novelty scraps
- ¾ yard total dark scraps
- 1¼ yards total light scraps
- 1⅜ yards bright multicoloured print
- 1½ yards black solid
- Backing 70" x 82"
- Batting 70" x 82"
- Neutral-colour all-purpose thread
- Quilting thread

Instructions
Note: *The sample uses one light print, one dark print and one novelty print for each block. For an extra scrappy quilt, try using a different print in every piece.*

Making Blocks
Step 1. Cut (40) 2⅞" x 2⅞" squares for E and (80) 2½" x 2½" squares for F from dark scraps. Cut E squares in half on one diagonal to make 80 E triangles.

Step 2. Prepare templates for A–D pieces using patterns given; cut as directed on each piece for one block. Repeat for 20 blocks.

Step 3. Sew a C triangle to each angled edge of B as shown in Figure 1; press seams toward C.

Figure 1

Figure 2

Step 4. Sew a B-C unit to each side of A as shown in Figure 2; press seams toward A.

Step 5. Sew D to F and DR to E as shown in Figure 3; press seams toward E and F. Join the units again referring to Figure 3.

Figure 3

Figure 4

Step 6. Sew a D-E-F unit to each side of the A-B-C unit to complete one block as shown in Figure 4; press seams toward D-E-F units. Repeat for 20 blocks.

Completing the Top
Step 1. Join blocks in five rows of four blocks each as shown in Figure 5; press seams in adjacent rows in opposite directions.

Make 5

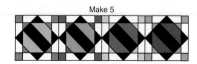

Figure 5

Step 2. Join rows to complete quilt centre; press seams in one direction.

Step 3. Cut and piece two 2½" x 60½" G strips and two 2½" x 52½" H strips black solid.

Step 4. Sew G to opposite sides, and H to the top and bottom of the pieced centre; press seams toward strips.

Step 5. Cut and piece four 6½" x 64½" bright multicoloured print I strips. Sew I to opposite sides, and top and bottom of the pieced centre to complete the quilt top; press seams toward I strips.

Finishing the Quilt

Step 1. Prepare quilt top for quilting and quilt referring to the General Instructions.

Step 2. When quilting is complete, trim batting and backing edges even with the quilted top.

Step 3. Cut seven 2¼" by fabric width strips binding fabric. Join strips on short ends to make one long strip. Fold the strip in half along length with wrong sides together; press.

Step 4. Sew binding to quilt edges, mitring corners and overlapping ends. Fold binding to the back side and stitch in place to finish. ✦

Random Colours
Placement Diagram 64" x 76"

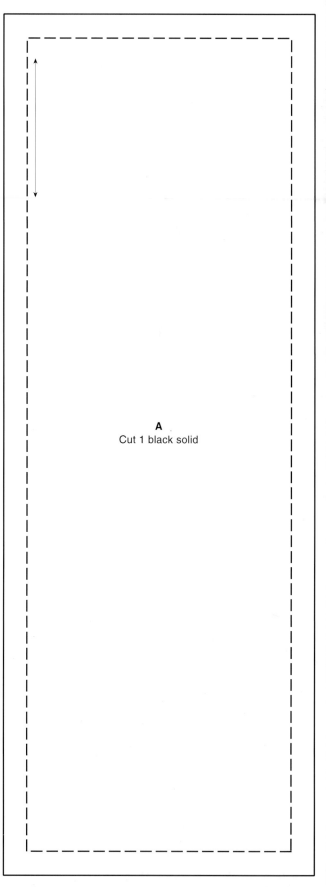

A
Cut 1 black solid

C
Cut 4 black solid

B
Cut 2 bright novelty scrap

D
Cut 8 light scrap
(reverse half for DR)

Metric Conversion Charts

yards	x	.9144	=	metres (m)
yards	x	91.44	=	centimetres (cm)
inches	x	2.54	=	centimetres (cm)
inches	x	25.40	=	millimetres (mm)
inches	x	.0254	=	metres (m)

centimetres	x	.3937	=	inches
metres	x	1.0936	=	yards

Standard Equivalents

⅛ inch	=	3.20 mm	=	0.32 cm
¼ inch	=	6.35 mm	=	0.635 cm
⅜ inch	=	9.50 mm	=	0.95 cm
½ inch	=	12.70 mm	=	1.27 cm
⅝ inch	=	15.90 mm	=	1.59 cm
¾ inch	=	19.10 mm	=	1.91 cm
⅞ inch	=	22.20 mm	=	2.22 cm
1 inch	=	25.40 mm	=	2.54 cm
⅛ yard	=	11.43 cm	=	0.11 m
¼ yard	=	22.86 cm	=	0.23 m
⅜ yard	=	34.29 cm	=	0.34 m
½ yard	=	45.72 cm	=	0.46 m
⅝ yard	=	57.15 cm	=	0.57 m
¾ yard	=	68.58 cm	=	0.69 m
⅞ yard	=	80.00 cm	=	0.80 m
1 yard	=	91.44 cm	=	0.91 m
1⅛ yard	=	102.87 cm	=	1.03 m
1¼ yard	=	114.30 cm	=	1.14 m
1⅜ yard	=	125.73 cm	=	1.26 m
1½ yard	=	137.16 cm	=	1.37 m
1⅝ yard	=	148.59 cm	=	1.49 m
1¾ yard	=	160.02 cm	=	1.60 m
1⅞ yard	=	171.44 cm	=	1.71 m
2 yards	=	182.88 cm	=	1.83 m

2⅛ yards	=	194.31 cm	=	1.94 m
2¼ yards	=	205.74 cm	=	2.06 m
2⅜ yards	=	217.17 cm	=	2.17 m
2½ yards	=	228.60 cm	=	2.29 m
2⅝ yards	=	240.03 cm	=	2.40 m
2¾ yards	=	251.46 cm	=	2.51 m
2⅞ yards	=	262.88 cm	=	2.63 m
3 yards	=	274.32 cm	=	2.74 m
3⅛ yards	=	285.75 cm	=	2.86 m
3¼ yards	=	297.18 cm	=	2.97 m
3⅜ yards	=	308.61 cm	=	3.09 m
3½ yards	=	320.04 cm	=	3.20 m
3⅝ yards	=	331.47 cm	=	3.31 m
3¾ yards	=	342.90 cm	=	3.43 m
3⅞ yards	=	354.32 cm	=	3.54 m
4 yards	=	365.76 cm	=	3.66 m
4⅛ yards	=	377.19 cm	=	3.77 m
4¼ yards	=	388.62 cm	=	3.89 m
4⅜ yards	=	400.05 cm	=	4.00 m
4½ yards	=	411.48 cm	=	4.11 m
4⅝ yards	=	422.91 cm	=	4.23 m
4¾ yards	=	434.34 cm	=	4.34 m
4⅞ yards	=	445.76 cm	=	4.46 m
5 yards	=	457.20 cm	=	4.57 m

INDEX

INDEX

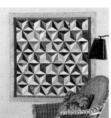

INDEX

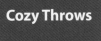